THE WORDS OF
ABRAHAM
LINCOLN

THE WORDS OF
ABRAHAM
LINCOLN

SELECTED AND WITH AN
INTRODUCTION BY
LARRY SHAPIRO

Newmarket Press
New York

The Newmarket "Words Of" Series

This book is published in the United States of America and Canada.

10 9 8 7 6 5 4 3 2 1 (pb)
10 9 8 7 6 5 4 3 2 1 (hc)

Library of Congress Cataloging-in-Publication Data

Lincoln, Abraham, 1809-1865.
  [Selections. 2009]
  The words of Abraham Lincoln / selected and with an introduction by
Larry Shapiro. — 1st ed.
    p. cm. — (The Newmarket "Words of" series)
  ISBN 978-1-55704-830-1 (pbk. : alk. paper) — ISBN 978-1-55704-
831-8 (hardcover : alk. paper) 1. Lincoln, Abraham, 1809-1865—Quota-
tions. 2. Lincoln, Abraham, 1809-1865—Oratory. 3. Lincoln, Abraham,
1809-1865—Language. 4. Presidents—United States—Quotations. I.
Shapiro, Larry, 1958- II. Title.
  E457.99.W67 2009
  973.7092—dc22

                                    2009002399

ISBN 978-1-55704-830-1 (paperback)
ISBN 978-1-55704-831-8 (hardcover)

QUANTITY PURCHASES
Companies, professional groups, clubs, and other organizations may
qualify for special terms when ordering quantities of this title. For
information, e-mail sales@newmarketpress.com or write to Special Sales,
Newmarket Press, 18 East 48th Street, New York, NY 10017; call
(212) 832-3575 ext. 19 or 1-800-669-3903; or fax (212) 832-3629

Manufactured in the United States of America

www.newmarketpress.com

CONTENTS

Portrait of Abraham Lincoln, February 9, 1864. Photograph by Anthony Berger of the Brady Studio.
(Courtesy of the Library of Congress, LC-DIG-ppmsca-19204)

INTRODUCTION

Larry Shapiro

"I have endured a great deal of ridicule without much malice; and have received a great deal of kindness, not quite free from ridicule. I am used to it."—Letter to James H. Hackett, November 2, 1863

In the spring of 1860, Abraham Lincoln wrote to the New York lawyer Charles C. Nott to thank him for editing the text of the Cooper Union Address in preparation for its publication. Nott had made some changes that he considered to be improvements in Lincoln's speech. "Of course," Lincoln wrote, "I would not object to, but would be pleased rather, with a more perfect edition of that speech." Having gotten his polite thanks out of the way, Lincoln went on to say, "Some of your notes I do not understand." Of one of Nott's changes, Lincoln wrote that "it would do little or no harm," although "it is not at all necessary to the sense I was trying to convey." Of another, grammatical change, Lincoln conceded that it "would certainly do no harm." Another proposed change, however, "would be a considerable blunder."

Lincoln summed up his attitude toward Nott's editing this way: "So far as it is intended merely to improve in grammar, and elegance of composition, I am quite agreed; but I do not wish the sense changed, or modified, to a hair's breadth. And you, not having studied the particular points so closely as I have, can not be quite sure that you do not change the sense when you do not intend it."

A few weeks before Lincoln reviewed Nott's editorial work, the one-term former Congressman from Illinois had become the Republican party's presidential candidate. The party had been in existence for only six years and Lincoln was far from a national figure. Presidential candidates were expected to avoid campaigning and speechmaking, so the publication of Lincoln's speech would be an important way to convey his ideas and his voice to voters. Considering Lincoln's limited education and his reputation as an unpolished country lawyer, we might expect him to have gratefully accepted Nott's help. Instead, it's possible that no author has ever told an editor to back off with more precision.

Although Lincoln could occasionally express uncertainty about his writing, throughout most of his life he was as confident in his use of language as in his political views. Among the few American presidents who became talented writers, Lincoln is the most improbable. Thomas Jefferson received a gentleman's education, corresponded with philosophers and scientists, and could write at leisure from his estate at Monticello. Theodore Roosevelt, in addition to his Harvard education, lived a life of adventure on the frontier West and wrote articles and books for audiences back East who were fascinated by the places he had been and the things he had done. Lincoln, whose parents were illiterate, was a self-taught lawyer, and busy throughout most of his adult life with the rough-and-tumble of politics. He never traveled to Europe, never saw the far West, and never aspired to be a writer in the sense that Jefferson and Theodore Roosevelt did. Language was a tool he learned from a few borrowed books and a lot of practical experience, an instrument of persuasion in courtrooms and a way to make himself trusted and liked in political meetings. He became well known for comical stories in which he was often the object of his humor. He liked to remind audiences of his humble origins. Lincoln was as skillful in his way of portraying himself as were Jefferson, the patrician philosopher, and Teddy Roosevelt, the big-game hunter and gentleman cowboy. "Nobody has ever expected me to be president," he wrote. "In my poor, lean, lank, face nobody has ever seen that there were any cabbages sprouting out."

But there were two ideas about which he wrote in deadly earnest: the significance of his rise as an example of how any free man in America could improve himself; and the need to protect this freedom against growing threats. These ideas, and the crisis in which they were tested, spurred Lincoln to become not just a wordsmith but a great writer.

The dividing line in Lincoln's writing, as in his political career, is May 1854, when Congress passed the

Kansas-Nebraska Act, which opened the door to an expansion of slavery beyond the South. Lincoln recognized that this changed the status of slavery from a peculiar local custom to a practice that could be justified anywhere in the United States. In his "Fragment on Slavery," written a few months later, Lincoln concluded that if it were possible to justify the enslavement of one person, it would be possible to justify enslaving anyone. There was no logical reason why the institution couldn't envelop people like himself and replace the principle that all men are created equal.

When Lincoln delivered the Cooper Union Address in New York City, he put aside the voice of the self-mocking country lawyer. He declared it was time for opponents of slavery to act upon their "moral, social, and political responsibilities." In January 1838, as a twenty-eight-year-old state legislator speaking to the Young Men's Lyceum of Springfield, Illinois, he had prophesied a crisis when the ideals of the founding fathers would be forgotten. When this happened, "Reason, cold, calculating, impassioned reason, must furnish all the materials for our future support and defense." That time had come, and Lincoln was prepared to claim the role of spokesman of reason. He didn't need advice from well-meaning New York lawyers about how it should be done.

As incoming president hoping to avoid civil war, Lincoln continued his appeal to reason: "My countrymen, one and all, think calmly and *well,* upon this whole subject," he wrote in the First Inaugural Address. Remonstrating with generals who were unable to perceive their advantages on the battlefield, he cited "maxims of war": "You seem to act as if this applies *against* you," he told McClellan, "but can not apply in your *favor.*"

But the generals had cause to wonder about the authority of this man who had previously mocked his own military experience, as did his political opponents and even allies, many of whom thought they were better qualified to lead, as well as the public, which had elected him president with 40 percent of the popular vote. Was this not the man who joked, "Nobody has ever expected me to be president"?

Lincoln's response was twofold. He minimized his own significance, but no longer in a humorous way: "I claim not to have controlled events, but confess plainly that events have controlled me." This, however, is no excuse for passivity: "Fellow citizens, *we* cannot escape history," he wrote at the end of 1862: "The fiery trial through which we pass, will light us down, in honor or dishonor, to the latest generation." It is a challenge beyond politics, beyond questions of ego: "We must disenthrall ourselves, and then we shall save our country." *Disenthrall* is a strange word choice, then as now, and it may have sent his audiences to their dictionaries. A secondary meaning of *enthrall* is "to enslave." Lincoln is approaching a theme he would sound throughout the remaining years of his life, that in fighting this war, we are not just freeing others in bondage, we are freeing ourselves. He later called it "a great national trial." In the spirit of a self-taught country lawyer who had become a great leader and writer, he wrote, "Let us, therefore, study the incidents of this, as philosophy to learn wisdom from, and none of them as wrongs to be revenged."

Two hundred years after his birth, Lincoln's writing endures, not only as documentation of his era but as "philosophy to learn wisdom from." We have organized the selections in this book to show Lincoln's progress from rustic politician to leader and healer of a wounded nation. The early writings reflect the outlook and ambitions of a self-made man. His interest in the backstage work of politics, in building alliances and outmaneuvering foes, is well represented in his letters, from the earliest campaigns to his presidential reprimand of New York powerbroker Thurlow Weed. His letters to Mary Todd Lincoln only hint at the tension and tragedy that shadowed their marriage, and reveal instead the equanimity Lincoln summoned to manage a difficult situation. In a letter to his improvident father, we see a foreshadowing of the way Lincoln would handle his erratic generals during the war.

It has often been remarked that no one who knew the politician of the 1840s would have predicted the greatness to come. But this is a man who knew how to use words as precise instruments to argue a position, to entertain people, to ridicule opponents, and occasionally to stir enthusiasm for his country. If there's no hint of greatness, neither is there any occasion that required it. Then Lincoln's letter of August 24, 1855, to his friend and confidant Joshua Speed raises the issue that would change his life. His memory of the captured slaves they saw on a boat trip has been "a continual torment," he tells Speed, "but I bite my lip and keep quiet." The time had come to break his silence.

In the years that followed, through the debates with Stephen Douglas and speeches like the Cooper Union Address, he became a master whose words could not be ignored. Lincoln's best-known writings are the major speeches from his presidential years: the Gettysburg Address, the First and Second Inaugural Addresses, the 1862 Annual Message to Congress. They speak to us today with undiminished urgency about leadership in a time of crisis, defining the national purpose, summoning people to make sacrifices for a greater good, and binding up a nation's wounds. As much as the Declaration of Independence, they are an essential part of America's identity and its legacy to the world.

—January 2009
New York City

Abraham Lincoln, August 13, 1860. Ambrotype photograph by
Preston Butler.
(Courtesy of the Library of Congress, LC-USZ62-7728A)

I. "Nobody Has Ever Expected Me to Be President"

FROM A LETTER TO JOSHUA SPEED
July 4, 1842

I am so poor, and make so little headway in the world, that I drop back in a month of idleness, as much as I gain in a year's rowing.

AUTOBIOGRAPHICAL SKETCH, 1859

By the winter of 1859, Abraham Lincoln was working quietly to win the Republican party's presidential nomination—propriety forbade a candidate to run openly for the nomination. He supplied this account of his early years to a Pennsylvania backer, who in turn passed it on to a political journalist. Expanded into a newspaper biography, the piece was much reprinted in Republican papers and helped Lincoln get the nomination at the Republican Convention the following June.

J. W. Fell, Esq   Springfield,
My dear Sir: Dec. 20. 1859

Herewith is a little sketch, as you requested. There is not much of it, for the reason, I suppose, that there is not much of me.

If any thing be made out of it, I wish it to be modest, and not to go beyond the material. If it were thought necessary to incorporate any thing from any of my speeches, I suppose there would be no objection. Of course it must not appear to have been written by myself. Yours very truly   A. Lincoln

I was born Feb. 12, 1809, in Hardin County, Kentucky. My parents were both born in Virginia, of undistinguished families—second families, perhaps I should say. My mother, who died in my tenth year, was of a family of the name of Hanks, some of whom now reside in Adams, and others in Macon counties, Illinois. My paternal grandfather, Abraham Lincoln, emigrated from Rockingham County, Virginia, to Kentucky, about 1781 or 2, where, a year or two later, he was killed by indians, not in battle, but by stealth, when [where?] he was laboring to open a farm in the forest. His ancestors, who were quakers, went to Virginia from Berks County, Pennsylvania. An effort to identify them with the New-England family of the same name ended in nothing more definite, than a similarity of Christian names in both families, such as Enoch, Levi, Mordecai, Solomon, Abraham, and the like.

My father, at the death of his father, was but six years of age; and he grew up, litterally without education. He removed from Kentucky to what is now Spencer county, Indiana, in my eighth year. We reached our new home about the time the State came into the Union. It was a wild region, with many bears and other wild animals still in the woods. There I grew up. There were some schools, so called; but no qualification was ever required of a teacher, beyond *"reading, writin, and cipherin,"* to the Rule of Three. If a straggler supposed to understand latin, happened to sojourn in the neighborhood, he was looked upon as a wizzard. There was absolutely nothing to excite ambition for education. Of course when I came of age I did not know much. Still somehow, I could read, write, and cipher to the Rule of Three; but that was all. I have not been to school since. The little advance I now have upon this store of education, I have picked up from time to time under the pressure of necessity.

I was raised to farm work, which I continued till I was twenty two. At twenty one I came to Illinois, and passed the first year in Illinois—Macon county. Then I got to New-Salem, (at that time in Sangamon, now in Menard county), where I remained a year as a sort of Clerk in a store. Then came the Black-Hawk war; and I was elected a Captain of Volunteers—a success which gave me more pleasure than any I have had since. I went the campaign, was elated, ran for the Legislature the same year (1832) and was beaten—the only time I have been beaten by the people. The next, and three succeeding biennial elections, I was elected to the Legislature. I was not a candidate afterwards. During this Legislative period I had studied law, and removed to Springfield to practice it. In 1846 I was once elected to the lower House of Congress. Was not a candidate for re-election. From 1849 to 1854, both inclusive, practiced law more assiduously than ever before. Always a whig in politics, and generally on the whig electoral tickets, making active canvasses. I was losing interest in politics, when the repeal of the Missouri Compromise aroused me again. What I have done since then is pretty well known.

If any personal description of me is thought desirable, it may be said, I am, in height, six feet, four inches, nearly; lean in flesh, weighing, on an average, one hundred and eighty pounds; dark complexion, with coarse black hair, and grey eyes—no other marks or brands recollected.   Yours very truly

A. LINCOLN

FROM A CAMPAIGN ANNOUNCEMENT, 1832
(Lincoln failed in his first attempt at a seat in the Illinois House of Representatives.)

Every man is said to have his peculiar ambition. Whether it be true or not, I can say for one that I have no other so great as that of being truly esteemed of my fellow men, by rendering myself worthy of their esteem. How far I shall succeed in gratifying this ambition, is yet to be developed. I am young and unknown to many of you. I was born and have ever remained in the most humble walks of life. I have no wealthy or popular relations to recommend me. My case is thrown exclusively upon the independent voters of this county, and if elected they will have conferred a favor upon me, for which I shall be unremitting in my labors to compensate. But if the good people in their wisdom shall see fit to keep me in the background, I have been too familiar with disappointments to be very much chagrined.

FROM A LETTER TO RICHARD S. THOMAS
February 14, 1843

By this point, the one-term state representative had set his sights higher, but failed to win the Whig Party nomination to run for the U.S. House of Representatives.

Friend Richard: . . . Now if you should hear any one say that Lincoln don't want to go to Congress, I wish you as a personal friend of mine, would tell him you have reason to believe he is mistaken. The truth is, I would like to go very much. Still, circumstances may happen which may prevent my being a candidate.

If there are any who be my friends in such an enterprise, what I now want is that they shall not throw me away just yet.

FROM A LETTER TO MARTIN S. MORRIS
April 14, 1843

It would astonish if not amuse, the older citizens of your County who twelve years ago knew me a strange[r], friendless, uneducated, penniless boy, working on a flat boat—at ten dollars per month to learn that I have been put down here as the candidate of pride, wealth, and arristocratic family distinction.

FROM A LETTER TO JOSEPHUS HEWITT
February 13, 1848
In 1846, Lincoln had been elected to the U.S. House of Representatives.

Your whig representative from Mississippi, P. W. Tompkins, has just shown me a letter of yours to him. I am jealous because you did not write to me. Perhaps you have forgotten me. Dont you remember a long black fellow who rode on horseback with you from Tremont to Springfield nearly ten years ago, swiming your horses over the Mackinaw on the trip? Well, I am that same one fellow yet.

FROM A LETTER TO WILLIAM H. HERNDON
January 8, 1848
Young Herndon was Lincoln's law partner and would one day be his biographer.

As to speechmaking, by way of getting the hang of the House I made a little speech two or three days ago on a post-office question of no general interest. I find speaking here and elsewhere about the same thing. I was about as badly scared, and no worse, as I am when I speak in court.

FROM A SPEECH IN THE U.S. HOUSE OF REPRESENTATIVES
January 12, 1848

The one-term Congressman would leave his mark on the U.S. House with a fiery denunciation of President Polk's conduct of the War with Mexico.

Some, if not all the gentlemen on, the other side of the House, who have addressed the committee within the last two days, have spoken rather complainingly, if I have rightly understood them, of the vote given a week or ten days ago, declaring that the war with Mexico was unnecessarily and unconstitutionally commenced by the President. I admit that such a vote should not be given, in mere party wantonness, and that the one given, is justly censurable, if it have no other, or better foundation. I am one of those who joined in that vote; and I did so under my best impression of the truth of the case. . . .

When the war began, it was my opinion that all those who, because of knowing too little, or because of knowing too much, could not conscientiously approve the conduct of the President, in the beginning of it, should, nevertheless, as good citizens and patriots, remain silent on that point, at least till the war should be ended. . . .

I carefully examined the President's messages, to ascertain what he himself had said and proved upon the point. The result of this examination was to make the impression, that taking for true, all the President states as facts, he falls far short of proving his justification; and that the President would have gone farther with his proof, if it had not been for the small matter, that the truth would not permit him. . . .

That originally having some strong motive—what, I will not stop now to give my opinion concerning—to involve the two countries in a war, and trusting to escape scrutiny, by fixing the public gaze upon the exceeding brightness of military glory—that attractive rainbow, that rises in showers of blood—that serpent's eye, that charms to destroy—he plunged into it, and has swept, on and on, till, disappointed in his calculation of the ease with which Mexico might be subdued, he now finds himself, he knows not where. How like the half insane mumbling of a fever-dream, is the whole war part of his late message!

As to the mode of terminating the war, and securing peace, the President is equally wandering and indefinite. . . . His mind, tasked beyond it's power, is running hither and thither, like some tortured creature, on a burning surface, finding no position, on which it can settle down, and be at ease.

FROM A LETTER TO MARY TODD LINCOLN
April 16, 1848

You know I told you in last Sunday's letter, I was going to make a little speech during the week; but the week has passed away without my getting a chance to do so; and now my interest in the subject has passed away too.

LETTER TO THOMAS LINCOLN AND JOHN D. JOHNSTON
December 24, 1848
Lincoln's letter to his father (who was illiterate) was written on the same paper as a letter to Lincoln's stepbrother Johnston.

My dear father:

Your letter of the 7th. was received night before last. I very cheerfully send you the twenty dollars, which sum you say is necessary to save your land from sale. It is singular that you should have forgotten a judgment against you; and it is more singular that the plaintiff should have let you forget it so long, particularly as I suppose you have always had property enough to satisfy a judgment of that amount. Before you pay it, it would be well to be sure you have not paid it; or, at least, that you can not prove you have paid it. Give my love to Mother, and all the connections. Affectionately your Son.

FROM A SPEECH AT KALAMAZOO, MICHIGAN
August 27, 1856

We are a great empire. We are eighty years old. We stand at once the wonder and admiration of the whole world, and we must enquire what it is that has given us so much prosperity, and we shall understand that to give up that one thing, would be to give up all future prosperity. This cause is that every man can make himself.

FROM THE SECOND LECTURE ON DISCOVERIES AND INVENTIONS, JACKSONVILLE, ILLINOIS
February 11, 1859

We have all heard of Young America. He is the most current youth of the age. Some think him conceited, and arrogant; but has he not reason to entertain a rather extensive opinion of himself? Is he not the inventor and owner of the present, and sole hope of the future?

FROM A SPEECH AT SPRINGFIELD, ILLINOIS
July 17, 1858
The object of Lincoln's ridicule is Democratic Senator Stephen Douglas, whom he hoped to unseat.

All the anxious politicians of his party, or who have been of his party for years past, have been looking upon him as certainly, at no distant day, to be the President of the United States. They have seen in his round, jolly, fruitful face, postoffices, landoffices, marshalships, and cabinet appointments, chargeships and foreign missions, bursting and sprouting out in wonderful exuberance ready to be laid hold of by their greedy hands.... On the contrary nobody has ever expected me to be President. In my poor, lean, lank, face, nobody has ever seen that any cabbages were sprouting out.

FROM A LETTER TO WILLIAM H. GRIGSBY
August 3, 1858

If you wish to be a lawyer, attach no consequence to the place you are in, or the person you are with; but get books, sit down anywhere, and go to reading for yourself. That will make a lawyer of you quicker than any other way.

FROM A LETTER TO ALEXANDER SYMPSON
December 12, 1858
Although Lincoln lost to Stephen Douglas, their debates would enlarge his reputation as spokesman for the Republican party.

I expect the result of the election went hard with you. So it did with me, too, perhaps not quite so hard as you may have supposed. I have an abiding faith that we shall beat them in the long run. Step by step the objects of the leaders will become too plain for the people to stand them. I write merely to let you know that I am neither dead nor dying.

Abraham Lincoln with his son Thomas (Tad), February 9, 1864.
Photograph by Anthony Berger of the Brady Studio.
(Courtesy of the Library of Congress, LC-USZ62-11897)

II. "I Hope This Letter Will Not Be Disagreeable to You": Courtship, Marriage, and Family

FROM A LETTER TO MRS. M. J. GREEN
September 22, 1860

Your kind congratulatory letter, of August, was
received in due course—and should have been
answered sooner. The truth is I have never corresponded much with ladies; and hence I postpone
writing letters to them, as a business which I do not
understand. I can only say now I thank you for the
good opinion you express of me, fearing, at the same
time, I may not be able to maintain it through life.

TWO LETTERS TO MARY S. OWENS
December 13, 1836
Lincoln considered marrying her without great enthusiasm.

Write back as soon as you get this, and if possible
say something that will please me, for really I have
not [been] pleased since I left you. This letter is so
dry and [stupid] that I am ashamed to send it, but
with my pres[ent feel]ings I can not do any better.

MAY 7, 1837

I am often thinking about what we said of your
coming to live at Springfield. I am afraid you would
not be satisfied. There is a great deal of flourishing
about in carriages here, which it would be your
doom to see without shareing in it. You would have
to be poor without the means of hiding your
poverty. Do you believe you could bear that
patiently? Whatever woman may cast her lot with

mine, should any ever do so, it is my intention to do all in my power to make her happy and contented; and there is nothing I can immagine, that would make me more unhappy than to fail in the effort.

FROM A LETTER TO JOHN STUART
January 23, 1841
His courtship of Mary Todd has apparently failed.

I am now the most miserable man living. If what I feel were equally distributed to the whole human family, there would not be one cheerful face on the earth. Whether I shall ever be better I can not tell; I awfully forebode I shall not. To remain as I am is impossible; I must die or be better, it appears to me.

FROM A LETTER TO JOSHUA SPEED
February 25, 1842
Lincoln and Speed, former business partners and house-mates, were pursuing brides at the same time and kept each other informed about their progress.

I now have no doubt that it is the peculiar misfortune of both you and me, to dream dreams of Elysium far exceeding all that any thing earthly can realize.

FROM A LETTER TO SAMUEL D. MARSHALL
November 11, 1842

Nothing new here, except my marrying, which to me, is matter of profound wonder.

FROM A LETTER TO JOSHUA SPEED
May 18, 1843

Are you possessing houses and lands, and oxen and asses, and men-servants and maid-servants, and begetting sons and daughters? We are not keeping house; but boarding at the Globe tavern, which is very well kept now by a widow lady of the name of Beck. Our room ... and boarding only costs four dollars a week.

FROM A LETTER TO JOSHUA SPEED
October 22, 1846

We have another boy, born the 10th. of March last. He is very much such a child as Bob was at his age—rather of a longer order. Bob is "short and low," and, I expect, always will be. He talks very plainly—almost as plainly as any body. He is quite smart enough. I some times fear he is one of the little rare-ripe sort, that are smarter at about five than ever after. He has a great deal of that sort of mischief, that is the off-spring of much animal spirits.

FROM LETTERS TO MARY TODD LINCOLN,
1848
Lincoln's law partner, William Herndon, is the principal source for stories about how Lincoln suffered in his marriage. But the bad feeling between Herndon and Mrs. Lincoln distorted his perceptions. These letters suggest that

Lincoln's marriage was too complex to be called good or bad. Lincoln himself wrote almost nothing about the marriage.

After being elected to Congress, Lincoln moved with his family to a boarding house in the District of Columbia. Mary subsequently left with the children to visit her family in Kentucky.

APRIL 16, 1848

Dear Mary:

In this troublesome world, we are never quite satisfied. When you were here, I thought you hindered me some in attending to business; but now, having nothing but business—no variety—it has grown exceedingly tasteless to me. I hate to sit down and direct documents, and I hate to stay in this old room by myself. . . .

I went yesterday to hunt the little plaid stockings, as you wished; but found that McKnight has quit business, and Allen had not a single pair of the description you give, and only one plaid pair of any sort that I thought would fit "Eddy's dear little feet." I have a notion to make another trial to-morrow morning. . . .

I wish you to enjoy yourself in every possible way; but is there no danger of wounding the feelings of your good father, by being so openly intimate with the Wickliffe family?

Mrs. Broome has not removed yet; but she thinks of doing so to-morrow. All the house—or rather, all with whom you were on decided good terms—send their love to you. The others say nothing.

Very soon after you went away, I got what I think a very pretty set of shirt-bosom studs— modest little ones, jet, set in gold, only costing 50 cents a piece, or 1.50 for the whole.

Suppose you do not prefix the "Hon" to the address on your letters to me any more. I like the letters very much, but I would rather they should not have that upon them. It is not necessary, as I suppose you have thought, to have them to come free.

And you are entirely free from head-ache? That is good—good—considering it is the first spring you have been free from it since we were acquainted. I am afraid you will get so well, and fat, and young, as to be wanting to marry again. Tell Louisa I want her to watch you a little for me. Get weighed, and write me how much you weigh.

I did not get rid of the impression of that foolish dream about dear Bobby till I got your letter written the same day. What did he and Eddy think of the little letters father sent them? Don't let the blessed fellows forget father.

JUNE 12, 1848

My Dear Wife:

On my return from Philadelphia, yesterday, where, in my anxiety I had been led to attend the whig convention I found your last letter. I was so tired and sleepy, having ridden all night, that I could not answer it till to-day; and now I have to do so in the H.R. The leading matter in your letter, is your wish to return to this side of the Mountains. Will you be a good girl in all things, if I consent? Then come along, and that as soon as possible. Having got the idea in my head, I shall be impatient till I see you. You will not have money enough to bring you; but I presume your uncle will supply you, and I will refund him here. By the way you do not mention whether you have received the fifty dollars I sent you. . . . I hope this letter will not be disagreeable to you; which, together with the circumstances under which I write, I hope will excuse me for not writing a longer one. Come on just as soon as you can. I want to see you, and our dear—dear boys very much. Every body here wants to see our dear Bobby.

Affectionately, A. Lincoln

AUGUST 8, 1863

My Dear Wife.

All as well as usual, and no particular trouble any way. I put the money into the Treasury at five per cent, with the previlege of withdrawing it any time upon thirty days' notice. I suppose you are glad to learn this. Tell dear Tad, poor "Nanny Goat," is lost; and Mrs. Cuthbert & I are in distress about it. The day you left Nanny was found resting herself, and chewing her little cud, on the middle of Tad's bed. But now she's gone! The gardener kept complaining that she destroyed the flowers, till it was concluded to bring her down to the White House. This was done, and the second day she had disappeared, and has not been heard of since. This is the last we know of poor "Nanny."

TELEGRAM
April 28, 1864

Tell Tad the goats and father are very well—especially the goats.

FROM A LETTER TO ULYSSES S. GRANT
January 19, 1865

Please read and answer this letter as though I was not President, but only a friend. My son, now in his twenty second year, having graduated at Harvard, wishes to see something of the war before it ends. I do not wish to put him in the ranks, nor yet to give him a commission, to which those who have already served long, are better entitled, and better qualified to hold. Could he, without embarrassment to you, or detriment to the service, go into your Military family with some nominal rank, I, and not the public, furnishing his necessary means? If no, say so without the least hesitation, because I am as anxious, and as deeply interested, that you shall not be encumbered as you can be yourself.

Abraham Lincoln, circa 1860. Albumen photograph by
Alexander Hesler.
(Courtesy of the Library of Congress, LC-DIG-ppmsca-19195)

III. "A Continual Torment": The Slavery Controversy

FRAGMENT ON SLAVERY, 1854

Lincoln's political silence lasted until the fall of 1854, a few months after this fragment was probably written, when he came forward to speak out against the possibility that slavery might be extended beyond the South until it became a national institution. At this point in his isolation, he was brooding about a custom he had disapproved of but considered politically "a minor question."

[JULY 1,1854?]

If A. can prove, however conclusively, that he may, of right, enslave B.—why may not B. snatch the same argument, and prove equally, that he may enslave A.?—

You say A. is white, and B. is black. It is *color,* then; the lighter, having the right to enslave the darker? Take care. By this rule, you are to be slave to the first man you meet, with a fairer skin than your own.

You do not mean *color* exactly?—You mean the whites are *intellectually* the superiors of the blacks, and, therefore have the right to enslave them? Take care again. By this rule, you are to be slave to the first man you meet, with an intellect superior to your own.

But, say you, it is a question of *interest;* and, if you can make it your *interest,* you have the right to enslave another. Very well. And if he can make it his interest, he has the right to enslave you.

27

FROM A LETTER TO JOSHUA SPEED, 1855

During the years of Lincoln's political exile the issue of slavery had intensified the differences between North and South. The issue of sectional difference takes on an unusually personal tone in this letter to Speed, who had been Lincoln's closest friend when both men lived in Illinois but who had since returned to his native Kentucky.

SPRINGFIELD, AUG. 24, 1855

Dear Speed:

You know what a poor correspondent I am. Ever since I received your very agreeable letter of the 22nd. of May I have been intending to write you in answer to it. You suggest that in political action now, you and I would differ. I suppose we would; not quite as much, however, as you may think. You know I dislike slavery; and you fully admit the abstract wrong of it. So far there is no cause of difference. But you say that sooner than yield your legal right to the slave—especially at the bidding of those who are not themselves interested, you would see the Union dissolved. I am not aware that *any one* is bidding you to yield that right; very certainly *I* am not. I leave that matter entirely to yourself. I also acknowledge *your* rights and *my* obligations, under the constitution, in regard to your slaves. I confess I hate to see the poor creatures hunted down, and caught, and carried back to their stripes, and unrewarded toils; but I bite my lip and keep quiet. In

1841 you and I had together a tedious low-water
trip, on a Steam Boat from Louisville to St. Louis.
You may remember, as I well do, that from
Louisville to the mouth of the Ohio there were, on
board, ten or a dozen slaves, shackled together with
irons. That sight was a continual torment to me; and
I see something like it every time I touch the Ohio,
or any other slave-border. It is hardly fair for you to
assume, that I have no interest in a thing which has,
and continually exercises, the power of making me
miserable. You ought rather to appreciate how much
the great body of the Northern people do crucify
their feelings, in order to maintain their loyalty to
the constitution and the Union.

FROM A LETTER TO GEORGE ROBERTSON, 1855

*Another Kentuckian, law professor George Robertson,
elicited a letter that reads like a rehearsal of the anti-
slavery rhetoric Lincoln was beginning to express in
public—including, in the final paragraph, an anticipa-
tion of the "House Divided" speech that would help make
Lincoln a national figure.*

You are not a friend of slavery in the abstract. In that
speech you spoke of *"the peaceful extinction of slavery"*
and used other expressions indicating your belief
that the thing was, at some time, to have an end[.]
Since then we have had thirty six years of experience;

and this experience has demonstrated, I think, that
there is no peaceful extinction of slavery in prospect
for us. The signal failure of Henry Clay, and other
good and great men, in 1849, to effect any thing in
favor of gradual emancipation in Kentucky, together
with a thousand other signs, extinguishes that hope
utterly. On the question of liberty, as a principle, we
are not what we have been. When we were the
political slaves of King George, and wanted to be
free, we called the maxim that "all men are created
equal" a self evident truth; but now when we have
grown fat, and have lost all dread of being slaves
ourselves, we have become so greedy to be *masters*
that we call the same maxim "a self-evident lie." The
fourth of July has not quite dwindled away; it is still
a great day—*for burning firecrackers* ! ! !

... So far as peaceful, voluntary emancipation is
concerned, the condition of the negro slave in
America, scarcely less terrible to the contemplation
of a free mind, is now as fixed, and hopeless of
change for the better, as that of the lost souls of the
finally impenitent. The Autocrat of all the Russias
will resign his crown, and proclaim his subjects free
republicans sooner than will our American masters
voluntarily give up their slaves.

Our political problem now is "Can we, as a nation, continue together *permanently—forever*—half
slave, and half free?" The problem is too mighty for
me. May God, in his mercy, superintend the solu-

tion. Your much obliged friend, and humble servant

A. LINCOLN

FROM THE SPEECH AT PEORIA
October 16, 1854

This is the prototype of the speech that made Lincoln a national figure and, six years later, President of the United States. In the years to come he would repeat, refine, and elaborate the speech hundreds of times, from frontier towns to The Cooper Union in New York City. On every occasion there was a personal target—Senator Stephen Douglas of Lincoln's home state, his old rival in politics and love, who was chief spokesman for the policy of accommodating the slaveholding states by permitting the extension of slavery to the North and the West. There was a political target, the Kansas-Nebraska Act of 1854, which opened the question of slavery to a vote in the Western territories. And there was a philosophical target, the notion that slavery was morally acceptable and consistent with the principles of the nation. In each speech, too, Lincoln would begin by trying to reassure the South that he wasn't advocating sudden abolition or any measures that might drive it out of the Union.

Before proceeding, let me say I think I have no prejudice against the Southern people. They are just what we would be in their situation. If slavery did not now exist amongst them, they would not introduce it. If it did now exist amongst us, we should not instantly give it up. This I believe of the masses north and south. Doubtless there are individuals, on both sides, who would not hold slaves under any circumstances; and others who would gladly introduce slavery anew, if it were out of existence. We know that some southern men do free their slaves, go north, and become tip-top abolitionists; while some northern ones go south, and become most cruel slave-masters.

When southern people tell us they are no more responsible for the origin of slavery, than we; I acknowledge the fact. When it is said that the institution exists; and that it is very difficult to get rid of it, in any satisfactory way, I can understand and appreciate the saying. I surely will not blame them for not doing what I should not know how to do myself. If all earthly power were given me, I should not know what to do, as to the existing institution. . . .

I trust I understand, and truly estimate the right of self-government. My faith in the proposition that each man should do precisely as he pleases with all which is exclusively his own, lies at the foundation of the sense of justice there is in me. I extend the principles to communities of men, as well as to individuals. I so extend it, because it is politically wise, as well as naturally just: politically wise, in saving us from broils about matters which do not concern us. Here, or at Washington, I would not trouble myself with the oyster laws of Virginia, or the cranberry laws of Indiana.

The doctrine of self government is right—absolutely and eternally right—but it has no just application, as here attempted. Or perhaps I should rather say that whether it has such just application depends upon whether a negro is *not* or *is* a man. If he is *not* a man, why in that case, he who *is* a man may, as a matter of self-government, do just as he pleases with him. But if the negro is a man, is it not to that extent, a total destruction of self-government, to say that he too shall not govern *himself?* When the white man governs himself that is self-government; but when he governs himself, and also governs *another* man, that is *more* than self-government—that is despotism. If the negro is a *man,* why then my ancient faith teaches me that "all men are created equal;" and that there can be no moral right in connection with one man's making a slave of another.

Judge Douglas frequently, with bitter irony and sarcasm, paraphrases our argument by saying "The white people of Nebraska are good enough to govern themselves, *but they are not good enough to govern a few miserable negroes!!*"

Well I doubt not that the people of Nebraska are, and will continue to be as good as the average of people elsewhere. I do not say the contrary. What I do say is, that no man is good enough to govern another man, *without that other's consent.* I say this is the leading principle—the sheet anchor of American republicanism....

ACCEPTANCE SPEECH AT THE ILLINOIS STATE CONVENTION, 1858: THE "HOUSE DIVIDED" PASSAGE

Lincoln continued to voice the conservative opposition to slavery—do nothing to interfere with slavery in the South, but nothing to encourage its extension or perpetuation— and in 1856 he made more than 50 speeches on behalf of the Republican party's first presidential candidate, John C. Frémont. In 1858, Lincoln was the new party's unanimous choice to run against Stephen Douglas for the U.S. Senate. The opening of his acceptance speech got the campaign off to an explosive start.

Mr. President and Gentlemen of the Convention.

If we could first know *where* we are, and *whither* we are tending, we could then better judge *what* to do, and *how* to do it.

We are now far into the *fifth* year, since a policy was initiated, with the *avowed* object, and *confident* promise, of putting an end to slavery agitation.

Under the operation of that policy, that agitation has not only, *not ceased,* but has *constantly augmented.*

In *my* opinion, it *will* not cease, until a *crisis* shall have been reached, and passed.

"A house divided against itself cannot stand."

I believe this government cannot endure, permanently half *slave* and half *free*.

I do not expect the Union to be *dissolved*—I do not expect the house to *fall*—but I *do* expect it will cease to be divided.

It will become *all* one thing, or *all* the other.

Either the *opponents* of slavery, will arrest the further spread of it, and place it where the public mind shall rest in the belief that it is in course of ultimate extinction; or its *advocates* will push it forward, till it shall become alike lawful in *all* the States, *old* as well as *new*—*North* as well as *South*.

Have we no *tendency* to the latter condition?

FROM THE FIRST DEBATE WITH DOUGLAS AT OTTAWA, ILLINOIS
August 21, 1858

Lincoln's lively campaign against Douglas reached its peak in the seven encounters in which they shared a platform and answered each other directly. Lincoln's chances of winning the election were slight, and he knew it. But he campaigned as if he understood that a larger prize than the Illinois Senate seat might be at stake. In the first debate, at Ottawa, Douglas opened and Lincoln followed in reply.

MY FELLOW-CITIZENS: When a man hears himself somewhat misrepresented, it provokes him—at least, I find it so with myself; but when the misrepresentation becomes very gross and palpable, it is more apt to amuse him. [Laughter.]....

Now gentlemen, I hate to waste my time on such things, but in regard to that general abolition tilt: that Judge Douglas makes, when he says that I was engaged at that time in selling out and abolitionizing the old Whig party——I hope you will permit me to read a part of a printed speech that I made then at Peoria, which will show altogether a different view of the position I took in that contest of 1854.

VOICE—Put on your specs.

MR. LINCOLN—Yes, sir, I am obliged to do so. I am no longer a young man. [Laughter.]....

Now gentlemen, I don't want to read at any greater length, but this is the true complexion of all I have ever said in regard to the institution of slavery and the black race. This is the whole of it, and anything that argues me into his idea of perfect social and political equality with the negro, is but a specious and fantastic arrangement of words, by which a man can prove a horse chestnut to be a chestnut horse. [Laughter.] I will say here, while upon this subject, that I have no purpose directly or indirectly to interfere with the institution of slavery in the States where it exists. I believe I have no lawful right to do so, and I have no inclination to do so....

Now I pass on to consider one or two more of these little follies....And so I think my friend, the

Judge, is equally at fault when he charges me at the time when I was in Congress of having opposed our soldiers who were fighting in the Mexican war. The Judge did not make his charge very distinctly but I can tell you what he can prove by referring to the record. You remember I was an old Whig, and whenever the Democratic party tried to get me to vote that the war had been righteously begun by the President, I would not do it. But whenever they asked for any money, or land warrants, or anything to pay the soldiers there, during all that time, I gave the same votes that Judge Douglas did. [Loud applause.] You can think as you please as to whether that was consistent. Such is the truth; and the Judge has the right to make all he can out of it. But when he, by a general charge, conveys the idea that I withheld supplies from the soldiers who were fighting in the Mexican war, or did anything else to hinder the soldiers, he is, to say the least, grossly and altogether mistaken, as a consultation of the records will prove to him.

. . . Henry Clay, my beau ideal of a statesman, the man for whom I fought all my humble life—Henry Clay once said of a class of men who would repress all tendencies to liberty and ultimate emancipation, that they must, if they would do this, go back to the era of our Independence, and muzzle the cannon which thunders its annual joyous return; they must blow out the moral lights around us; they must penetrate the human soul, and eradicate there the love of liberty; and then and not till then, could they perpetuate slavery in this country! [Loud cheers.] To my thinking, Judge Douglas is, by his example and vast influence, doing that very thing in this community, [cheers] when he says that the negro has nothing in the Declaration of Independence. Henry Clay plainly understood the contrary. Judge Douglas is going back to the era of our Revolution, and to the extent of his ability, muzzling the cannon which thunders its annual joyous return. When he invites any people willing to have slavery, to establish it, he is blowing out the moral lights around us. [Cheers.] When he says he "cares not whether slavery is voted down or voted up,"—that it is a sacred right of self government—he is in my judgment penetrating the human soul and eradicating the light of reason and the love of liberty in this American people. [Enthusiastic and continued applause.]

FROM THE COOPER UNION ADDRESS
February 27, 1860
After losing to Douglas, Lincoln continued to speak out against the extension of slavery, and in early 1860, the presidential election year, he made a crucial speaking tour of the East Coast. His most important stop was at the Cooper Union in New York City, where his audience was probably the most influential he had ever addressed. Lincoln's speech was an impassioned advocacy of the middle

ground: do nothing to encourage slavery, but nothing to in-terfere with the institution where it already existed.

If slavery is right, all words, acts, laws, and constitutions against it, are themselves wrong, and should be silenced, and swept away. If it is right, we cannot justly object to its nationality—its universality; if it is wrong, they cannot justly insist upon its extension—its enlargment. All they ask, we could readily grant, if we thought slavery right; all we ask, they could as readily grant, if they thought it wrong. Their thinking it right, and our thinking it wrong, is the precise fact upon which depends the whole controversy. Thinking it right, as they do, they are not to blame for desiring its full recognition, as being right; but, thinking it wrong, as we do, can we yield to them? Can we cast our votes with their view, and against our own? In view of our moral, social, and political responsibilities, can we do this?

Wrong as we think slavery is, we can yet afford to let it alone where it is, because that much is due to the necessity arising from its actual presence in the nation; but can we, while our votes will prevent it, allow it to spread into the National Territories, and to overrun us here in these Free States? If our sense of duty forbids this, then let us stand by our duty, fearlessly and effectively. Let us be diverted by none of those sophistical contrivances wherewith we are so industriously plied and belabored—contrivances such as groping for some middle ground between the right and the wrong, vain as the search for a man who should be neither a living man nor a dead man—such as a policy of "don't care" on a question about which all true men do care—such as Union appeals beseeching true Union men to yield to Disunionists, reversing the divine rule, and calling, not the sinners, but the righteous to repentance—such as invocations to Washington, imploring men to unsay what Washington said, and undo what Washington did.

Neither let us be slandered from our duty by false accusations against us, nor frightened from it by menaces of destruction to the Government nor of dungeons to ourselves. LET US HAVE FAITH THAT RIGHT MAKES MIGHT, AND IN THAT FAITH, LET US, TO THE END, DARE TO DO OUR DUTY AS WE UNDERSTAND IT.

LETTER TO MARY TODD LINCOLN, 1860

[EXETER, N.H. MARCH 4,1860]

I have been unable to escape this toil. If I had foreseen it, I think I would not have come east at all. The speech at New York, being within my calculation before I started, went off passably well and gave me no trouble whatever. The difficulty was to make nine others, before reading audiences who had already seen all my ideas in print.

Portrait of Abraham Lincoln, January 8, 1864. Albumen photograph by
Mathew B. Brady.
(Courtesy of the Library of Congress, LC-DIG-ppmsca-19211)

IV. "Essentially a People's Contest": The War Begins

FAREWELL ADDRESS, SPRINGFIELD, 1861
February 11, 1861

Lincoln delivered these remarks from the rear platform of a train that would take him to Washington, D.C. Now President-elect, he had been out of office more than ten years and had never held an executive position. But there's little sense of triumph in his farewell.

My friends—No one, not in my situation, can appreciate my feeling of sadness at this parting. To this place, and the kindness of these people, I owe every thing. Here I have lived a quarter of a century, and have passed from a young to an old man. Here my children have been born, and one is buried. I now leave, not knowing when, or whether ever, I may return, with a task before me greater than that which rested upon Washington. Without the assistance of that Divine Being, who ever attended him, I cannot succeed. With that assistance I cannot fail. Trusting in Him, who can go with me, and remain with you and be every where for good, let us confidently hope that all will yet be well. To His care commending you, as I hope in your prayers you will commend me, I bid you an affectionate farewell.

REPLY TO GOVERNOR OLIVER P. MORTON AT INDIANAPOLIS, INDIANA
February 11, 1861

In all the trying positions in which I shall be placed, and doubtless I shall be placed in many trying ones, my reliance will be placed upon you and the people of the United States—and I wish you to remember now and forever, that it is your business, and not mine; that if the union of these States, and the liberties of this people, shall be lost, it is but little to any one man of fifty-two years of age, but a great deal to the thirty millions of people who inhabit these United States, and to their posterity in all coming time. It is your business to rise up and preserve the Union and liberty, for yourselves, and not for me. I desire they shall be constitutionally preserved.

I, as already intimated, am but an accidental instrument, temporary, and to serve but for a limited time, but I appeal to you again to constantly bear in mind that with you, and not with politicians, not with Presidents, not with office-seekers, but with you, is the question, "Shall the Union and shall the liberties of this country be preserved to the latest generation?"

SPEECH AT INDEPENDENCE HALL, PHILADELPHIA, 1861

In the period between his election and his inauguration Lincoln avoided saying anything that might provoke the South into rebellion, and on his journey from Springfield to Washington he tried to say nothing at all about the nation's crisis. But when he stopped in Philadelphia, he learned that there was a plot to assassinate him in Balti-

*more, and at Independence Hall he was stirred by the pres-
ence of a symbol he held sacred.*

FEBRUARY 22, 1861

Mr. CUYLER:—I am filled with deep emotion at
finding myself standing here in the place where were
collected together the wisdom, the patriotism, the
devotion to principle, from which sprang the institutions under which we live. You have kindly sug-
gested to me that in my hands is the task of
restoring peace to our distracted country. I can say in
return, sir, that all the political sentiments I entertain have been drawn, so far as I have been able to
draw them, from the sentiments which originated,
and were given to the world from this hall in which
we stand. I have never had a feeling politically that
did not spring from the sentiments embodied in the
Declaration of Independence. (Great cheering.) I
have often pondered over the dangers which were in-
curred by the men who assembled here and adopted
that Declaration of Independence—I have pondered
over the toils that were endured by the officers and
soldiers of the army, who achieved that Independence. (Applause.) I have often inquired of myself,
what great principle or idea it was that kept this
Confederacy so long together. It was not the mere
matter of the separation of the colonies from the
mother land; but something in that Declaration giving liberty, not alone to the people of this country,

but hope to the world for all future time. (Great applause.) It was that which gave promise that in due time the weights should be lifted from the shoulders of all men, and that *all* should have an equal chance. (Cheers.) This is the sentiment embodied in that Declaration of Independence.

Now, my friends, can this country be saved upon that basis? If it can, I will consider myself one of the happiest men in the world if I can help to save it. If it can't be saved upon that principle, it will be truly awful. But, if this country cannot be saved without giving up that principle—I was about to say I would rather be assassinated on this spot than to surrender it. (Applause.)

Now, in my view of the present aspect of affairs, there is no need of bloodshed and war. There is no necessity for it. I am not in favor of such a course, and I may say in advance, there will be no blood shed unless it be forced upon the Government. The Government will not use force unless force is used against it. (Prolonged applause and cries of "That's the proper sentiment.")

My friends, this is a wholly unprepared speech. I did not expect to be called upon to say a word when I came here—I supposed I was merely to do something towards raising a flag. I may, therefore, have said something indiscreet, (cries of "no, no"), but I have said nothing but what I am willing to live by, and, in the pleasure of Almighty God, die by.

FROM THE FIRST INAUGURAL ADDRESS, 1861

Could a speech save the Union? Lincoln began work on his First Inaugural before leaving Springfield, and in Washington he consulted with Douglas and Seward in an attempt to assemble as many compelling reasons as possible why the South should not secede.

March 4, 1861

Fellow citizens of the United States:

In compliance with a custom as old as the government itself, I appear before you to address you briefly, and to take, in your presence, the oath prescribed by the Constitution of the United States, to be taken by the President "before he enters on the execution of his office."

I do not consider it necessary, at present, for me to discuss those matters of administration about which there is no special anxiety, or excitement.

Apprehension seems to exist among the people of the Southern States, that by the accession of a Republican Administration, their property, and their peace, and personal security, are to be endangered. There has never been any reasonable cause for such apprehension. Indeed, the most ample evidence to the contrary has all the while existed, and been open to their inspection. It is found in nearly all the published speeches of him who now addresses you....

Physically speaking, we cannot separate. We cannot remove our respective sections from each other, nor build an impassable wall between them. A husband and wife may be divorced, and go out of the presence, and beyond the reach of each other; but the different parts of our country cannot do this. They cannot but remain face to face; and intercourse, either amicable or hostile, must continue between them. Is it possible then to make that intercourse more advantageous, or more satisfactory, *after* separation than *before?* Can aliens make treaties easier than friends can make laws? Can treaties be more faithfully enforced between aliens, than laws can among friends? Suppose you go to war, you cannot fight always; and when, after much loss on both sides, and no gain on either, you cease fighting, the identical old questions, as to terms of intercourse, are again upon you.

This country, with its institutions, belongs to the people who inhabit it. Whenever they shall grow weary of the existing government, they can exercise their *constitutional* right of amending it, or their *revolutionary* right to dismember, or overthrow it. I can not be ignorant of the fact that many worthy, and patriotic citizens are desirous of having the national constitution amended. While I make no recommendation of amendments, I fully recognize the rightful authority of the people over the whole subject, to be exercised in either of the modes prescribed in the instrument itself; and I should, under existing circumstances, favor, rather than oppose, a fair opportunity being afforded the people to act upon it....

My countrymen, one and all, think calmly and *well,* upon this whole subject. Nothing valuable can be lost by taking time. If there be an object to *hurry* any of you, in hot haste, to a step which you would never take *deliberately,* that object will be frustrated by taking time; but no good object can be frustrated by it. Such of you as are now dissatisfied, still have the old Constitution unimpaired, and, on the sensitive point, the laws of your own framing under it; while the new administration will have no immediate power, if it would, to change either. If it were admitted that you who are dissatisfied, hold the right side in the dispute, there still is no single good reason for precipitate action. Intelligence, patriotism, Christianity, and a firm reliance on Him, who has never yet forsaken this favored land, are still competent to adjust, in the best way, all our present difficulty.

In *your* hands, my dissatisfied fellow countrymen, and not in *mine,* is the momentous issue of civil war. The government will not assail *you.* You can have no conflict, without being yourselves the aggressors. *You* have no oath registered in Heaven to destroy the government, while *I* shall have the most solemn one to "preserve, protect and defend" it.

I am loth to close. We are not enemies, but friends. We must not be enemies. Though passion may have strained, it must not break our bonds of affection. The mystic chords of memory, stretching from every battle-field, and patriot grave, to every living heart and hearthstone, all over this broad land, will yet swell the chorus of the Union, when again touched, as surely they will be, by the better angels of our nature.

FROM THE MESSAGE TO CONGRESS IN SPECIAL SESSION
July 1861

When the war came, Lincoln took care to define it as a war of democracy against despotism, "a people's contest," instead of a war against slavery. As a practical matter, the President wanted to retain the loyalty of slaveholding border states that hadn't seceded, and he wanted to make it as easy as possible for rebellious states to end their rebellion. But at this point Lincoln also still held to his conviction that slavery should not be abolished abruptly because of the economic consequences and what he imagined would be insoluble social problems.

And the issue embraces more than the fate of these United States. It presents to the whole family of man, the question, whether a constitutional republic, or a democracy—a government of the people, by the same people—can, or cannot, maintain its territorial integrity, against its own domestic foes. It presents the question, whether discontented individuals, too few in numbers to control administration, according to organic law, in any case, can always, upon the pretences made in this case, or on any other pretences, or arbitrarily, without any pretence, break up their Government, and thus practically put an end to free government upon the earth. It forces us to ask: "Is there, in all republics, this inherent, and fatal weakness?" "Must a government, of necessity, be too strong for the liberties of its own people, or too weak to maintain its own existence?" . . .

This is essentially a People's contest. On the side of the Union, it is a struggle for maintaining in the world, that form, and substance of government, whose leading object is, to elevate the condition of men—to lift artificial weights from all shoulders—to clear the paths of laudable pursuit for all—to afford all, an unfettered start, and a fair chance, in the race of life. Yielding to partial, and temporary departures, from necessity, this is the leading object of the government for whose existence we contend.

I am most happy to believe that the plain people understand, and appreciate this. It is worthy of note, that while in this, the government's hour of trial, large numbers of those in the Army and Navy, who have been favored with the offices, have resigned, and proved false to the hand which had pampered them, not one common soldier, or common sailor is known to have deserted his flag.

LETTER TO COLONEL ELLSWORTH'S PARENTS, 1861

Throughout the war, Lincoln's letters of condolence helped to establish his image as a compassionate leader and to off-set newspaper portrayals of him as a bungler who didn't care how many lives he sacrificed. Colonel Elmer Ellsworth, the first commissioned officer to be killed in the war, was shot by a hotel keeper in Alexandria, Virginia, while trying to remove a Confederate flag from the roof of the hotel. He had been a clerk in Lincoln's law office in Springfield and had accompanied Lincoln on the train to Washington.

To the Father and Mother of Col.   Washington D.C.
Elmer E. Ellsworth: May 25. 1861

My dear Sir and Madam, In the untimely loss of your noble son, our affliction here, is scarcely less than your own. So much of promised usefulness to one's country, and of bright hopes for one's self and friends, have rarely been so suddenly dashed, as in his fall. In size, in years, and in youthful appearance, a boy only, his power to command men, was surpassingly great. This power, combined with a fine intellect, an indomitable energy, and a taste altogether military, constituted in him, as seemed to me, the best natural talent, in that department, I ever knew.

And yet he was singularly modest and deferential in social intercourse. My acquaintance with him began less than two years ago; yet through the latter half of the intervening period, it was as intimate as the disparity of our ages, and my engrossing engagements, would permit. To me, he appeared to have no indulgences or pastimes; and I never heard him utter a profane, or an intemperate word. What was conclusive of his good heart, he never forgot his parents. The honors he labored for so laudably, and, in the sad end, so gallantly gave his life, he meant for them, no less than for himself.

In the hope that it may be no intrusion upon the sacredness of your sorrow, I have ventured to address you this tribute to the memory of my young friend, and your brave and early fallen child.

May God give you that consolation which is beyond all earthly power. Sincerely your friend in a common affliction—   A. LINCOLN

LETTER TO COUNT A. de GASPARIN, 1862

The Union and the Confederacy were also engaged in a diplomatic war for the support of European governments. One major European supporter of the Union cause, Count de Gasparin, had expressed wonder that the North didn't make better use of its numerical superiority. Lincoln's answer explains the strategic problems, but also reminds the Count that as a democratic government the Union faced special difficulties in mobilizing resources.

Executive Mansion   Washington August 4, 1862

Dear Sir: Your very acceptable letter dated Orbe Canton de Vaud, Switzerland 18th of July 1862 is received. The moral effect was the worst of the affair before Richmond; and that has run its course downward; we are now at a stand, and shall soon be rising again, as we hope. I believe it is true that in men and material, the enemy suffered more than we, in that series of conflicts; while it is certain he is less able to bear it.

With us every soldier is a man of character and must be treated with more consideration than is customary in Europe. Hence our great army for slighter causes than could have prevailed there has dwindled rapidly, bringing the necessity for a new call, earlier than was anticipated. We shall easily obtain the new levy, however. Be not alarmed if you shall learn that we shall have resorted to a draft for part of this. It seems strange, even to me, but it is true, that the Government is now pressed to this course by a popular demand. Thousands who wish not to personally enter the service are nevertheless anxious to pay and send substitutes, provided they can have assurance that unwilling persons similarly situated will be compelled to do like wise. Besides this, volunteers mostly choose to enter newly forming regiments, while drafted men can be sent to fill up the old ones, wherein, man for man, they are quite doubly as valuable.

You ask "why is it that the North with her great armies, so often is found, with inferiority of numbers, face to face with the armies of the South?" While I painfully know the fact, a military man, which I am not, would better answer the question. The fact I know, has not been overlooked; and I suppose the cause of its continuance lies mainly in the other facts that the enemy holds the interior, and we the exterior lines; and that we operate where the people convey information to the enemy, while he operates where they convey none to us.

I have received the volume and letter which you did me the honor of addressing to me, and for which please accept my sincere thanks. You are much admired in America for the ability of your writings, and much loved for your generosity to us, and your devotion to liberal principles generally.

You are quite right, as to the importance to us, for its bearing upon Europe, that we should achieve military successes; and the same is true for us at home as well as abroad. Yet it seems unreasonable that a series of successes, extending through half-a-year, and clearing more than a hundred thousand square miles of country, should help us so little, while a single half-defeat should hurt us so much. But let us be patient.

I am very happy to know that my course has not conflicted with your judgement, of propriety and policy.

I can only say that I have acted upon my best convictions without selfishness or malice, and that by the help of God, I shall continue to do so.

Please be assured of my highest respect and esteem.

LETTER TO HORACE GREELEY, 1862

Not every Northerner was satisfied with Lincoln's vision of the war as "a people's contest." Greeley, editor of the New York Tribune, had attacked Lincoln in his paper for not fighting the war to abolish slavery. Although Lincoln had already prepared a statement on emancipation and was awaiting an occasion to issue it, such as a major Union victory, he answered Greeley by insisting that there was a larger issue than slavery at stake in the war.

Hon. Horace Greeley: Executive Mansion,
Dear Sir   Washington, August 22, 1862.

I have just read yours of the 19th. addressed to myself through the New-York Tribune....

As to the policy I "seem to be pursuing" as you say, I have not meant to leave any one in doubt.

I would save the Union. I would save it the shortest way under the Constitution. The sooner the national authority can be restored; the nearer the Union will be "the Union as it was." If there be those who would not save the Union, unless they could at the same time *save* slavery, I do not agree with them. If there be those who would not save the

Union unless they could at the same time *destroy* slavery, I do not agree with them. My paramount object in this struggle is to save the Union, and is *not* either to save or to destroy slavery. If I could save the Union without freeing *any* slave I would do it, and if I could save it by freeing *all* the slaves I would do it; and if I could save it by freeing some and leaving others alone I would also do that. What I do about slavery, and the colored race, I do because I believe it helps to save the Union; and what I forbear, I forbear because I do *not* believe it would help to save the Union. I shall do *less* whenever I shall believe what I am doing hurts the cause, and I shall do *more* whenever I shall believe doing more will help the cause. I shall try to correct errors when shown to be errors; and I shall adopt new views so fast as they shall appear to be true views.

I have here stated my purpose according to my view of *official* duty; and I intend no modification of my oft-expressed *personal* wish that all men every where could be free.   Yours,

A. LINCOLN

Lincoln meeting with General George B. McClellan (third from left) and other officers at McClellan's headquarters near Antietam, Maryland, October 3, 1862. Detail of photograph by Alexander Gardner. *(Courtesy of the Library of Congress, LC-DIG-cwpb-04352)*

V. "Maxims of War": Lincoln to His Generals

LETTER TO GENERAL DON CARLOS BUELL, 1862

Lincoln, whose experience in the military was limited to three months in a militia troop during a brief Indian war, when the only enemy he saw wandered into camp by mistake, had to think about strategy and tactics for the first time when he became commander-in-chief. Because he was dealing with sensitive egos and even with a potential rival in George Mc Clellan, he also had to become a psychologist of the military mind. This letter to General Buell, commander of the theater that included most of Kentucky, contains some basic theorizing by the novice military strategist.

copy—one also sent to Gen. Halleck.

Brig. Genl. Buell.   Executive Mansion,
My dear Sir: Washington, Jan. 13, 1862.

Your despatch of yesterday is received, in which you say "I have received your letter and Gen. Mc-Clellan's; and will, at once devote all my efforts to your views, and his." In the midst of my many cares, I have not seen, or asked to see, Gen. McClellan's letter to you. For my own views, I have not offered, and do not now offer them as orders; and while I am glad to have them respectfully considered, I would blame you to follow them contrary to your own clear judgment—unless I should put them in the form of orders. As to Gen. McClellan's views, you understand your duty in regard to them better than I do. With this preliminary, I state my general idea of this war to be that we have the *greater* numbers, and the enemy has the *greater* facility of concentrating forces upon points of collision; that we must fail, unless we can find some way of making *our* advantage an over-match for *his;* and that this can only be done by menacing him with superior forces at *different* points, at the *same* time; so that we can safely attack, one, or both, if he makes no change; and if he *weakens* one to *strengthen* the other, forbear to attack the strengthened one, but seize, and hold the weakened one, gaining so much. To illustrate, suppose last summer, when Winchester ran away to re-inforce Mannassas, we had forborne to attack Mannassas, but had seized and held Winchester. I mention this to illustrate, and not to criticise. I did not lose confidence in Mc-Dowell, and I think less harshly of Patterson than some others seem to. In application of the general rule I am suggesting, every particular case will have its modifying circumstances, among which the most constantly present, and most difficult to meet, will be the want of perfect knowledge of the enemies' movements. This had it's part in the Bull-Run case; but worse, in that case, was the expiration of the terms of the three months men. Applying the principle to your case, my idea is that Halleck shall menace Columbus, and "down river" generally; while you menace Bowling-Green, and East Tennessee. If the enemy shall concentrate at Bowling-Green, do not retire from his front; yet do not fight him there, either, but seize Columbus and East Tennessee, one or both, left exposed by the concentration at Bowling Green. It is matter of no small anxiety to me and one which I am sure you will not over-look, that the East Tennessee line, is so long, and over so bad a road.

Yours very truly
A. LINCOLN

LETTER TO GENERAL GEORGE McCLELLAN
February 3, 1862

At issue was the campaign against Richmond. Lincoln favored a direct advance south from Washington, while McClellan devised a more complicated attack by land and water. The President allowed the general to have his way.

Major General McClellan   Executive Mansion,
My dear Sir: Washington, Feb. 3, 1862.

You and I have distinct, and different plans for a movement of the Army of the Potomac—yours to be down the Chesapeake, up the Rappahannock to Urbana, and across land to the terminus of the Railroad on the York River—, mine to move directly to a point on the Railroad South West of Manassas.

If you will give me satisfactory answers to the following questions, I shall gladly yield my plan to yours.

1st. Does not your plan involve a greatly larger expenditure of *time,* and *money* than mine?

2nd. Wherein is a victory *more certain* by your plan than mine?

3rd. Wherein is a victory *more valuable* by your plan than mine?

4th. In fact, would it not be *less* valuable, in this, that it would break no great line of the enemie's communications, while mine would?

5th. In case of disaster, would not a safe retreat be more difficult by your plan than by mine?

Yours truly

A. LINCOLN

LETTER TO GENERAL McCLELLAN
April 9, 1862

McClellan's plans for the Peninsular campaign led to another disagreement with Lincoln over whether the general was leaving enough troops to defend Washington and whether the President was allowing enough troops for the general to carry out his plan.

Major General McClellan.   Washington,
My dear Sir.   April 9. 1862

Your despatches complaining that you are not properly sustained, while they do not offend me, do pain me very much.

Blencker's Division was withdrawn from you before you left here; and you knew the pressure under which I did it, and, as I thought, acquiesced in it—certainly not without reluctance.

After you left, I ascertained that less than twenty thousand unorganized men, without a single field battery, were all you designed to be left for the defence of Washington, and Manassas Junction; and part of this even, was to go to Gen. Hooker's old position. Gen. Banks' corps, once designed for Manassas Junction, was diverted, and tied up on the line of Winchester and Strausburg, and could not leave it without again exposing the upper Potomac, and the Baltimore and Ohio Railroad. This presented, (or would present, when McDowell and Sumner should be gone) a great temptation to the enemy to turn back from the Rappahanock, and sack Washington. My explicit order that Washington should, by the judgment of all the commanders of Army corps, be left entirely secure, had been neglected. It was precisely this that drove me to detain McDowell.

I do not forget that I was satisfied with your arrangement to leave Banks at Mannassas Junction; but when that arrangement was broken up, and nothing was substituted for it, of course I was not satisfied. I was constrained to substitute something for it myself. And now allow me to ask "Do you really think I should permit the line from Richmond, via Mannassas Junction, to this city to be entirely open, except what resistance could be presented by less than twenty thousand unorganized troops?" This is a question which the country will not allow me to evade.

There is a curious mystery about the number of the troops now with you. When I telegraphed you on the 6th. saying you had over a hundred thousand with you, I had just obtained from the Secretary of War, a statement, taken as he said, from your own returns, making 108,000 then with you, and en route to you. You now say you will have but 85,000, when all en route to you shall have reached you. How can the discrepancy of 23,000 be accounted for?

As to Gen. Wool's command, I understand it is doing for you precisely what a like number of your own would have to do, if that command was away.

I suppose the whole force which has gone forward for you, is with you by this time; and if so, I think it is the precise time for you to strike a blow. By delay the enemy will relatively gain upon you—that is, he will gain faster, by fortifications and re-inforcements, than you can by re-inforcements alone.

And, once more let me tell you, it is indispensable to *you* that you strike a blow. *I* am powerless to help this. You will do me the justice to remember I always insisted, that going down the Bay in search of a field, instead of fighting at or near Mannassas, was only shifting, and not surmounting, a difficulty—that we would find the same enemy, and the same, or equal, intrenchments, at either place. The country will not fail to note—is now noting—that the present hesitation to move upon an intrenched enemy, is but the story of Manassas repeated.

I beg to assure you that I have never written you, or spoken to you, in greater kindness of feeling than now, nor with a fuller purpose to sustain you, so far as in my most anxious judgment, I consistently can. *But you must act.* Yours very truly   A. LINCOLN

LETTER TO GENERAL McCLELLAN
July 2, 1862
Within a few miles of Richmond, McClellan was attacked
and driven southward. In turning down the general's re-
quest for 50,000 more troops, Lincoln was careful not to
blame him for failure, although within a few days he
would replace McClellan with Henry W. Halleck as chief
of all the Federal armies.

Washington, D.C.,

Major Gen. McClellan   July 2 1862.

Your despatch of Tuesday morning induces me
to hope your Army is having some rest. In this hope,
allow me to reason with you a moment. When you
ask for fifty thousand men to be promptly sent you,
you surely labor under some gross mistake of fact.
Recently you sent papers showing your disposal of
forces, made last spring, for the defence of Washington, and advising a return to that plan. I find it
included in, and about Washington seventy-five
thousand men. Now please be assured, I have not
men enough to fill that very plan by fifteen thousand. All of Fremont in the valley, all of Banks, all of
McDowell, not with you, and all in Washington,
taken together do not exceed, if they reach sixty
thousand. With Wool and Dix added to those
mentioned, I have not, outside of your Army,
seventy-five thousand men East of the mountains.
Thus, the idea of sending you fifty thousand, or any
other considerable force promptly, is simply absurd.

If in your frequent mention of responsibility, you have the impression that I blame you for not doing more than you can, please be relieved of such impression. I only beg that in like manner, you will not ask impossibilities of me. If you think you are not strong enough to take Richmond just now, I do not ask you to try just now. Save the Army, material and personal; and I will strengthen it for the offensive again, as fast as I can. The Governors of eighteen states offer me a new levy of three hundred thousand, which I accept.

A. LINCOLN

TWO LETTERS TO GENERAL McCLELLAN, 1862

The victory at Antietam was a major turning point for the Union Army, but McClellan complained afterward of supply and transportation problems and failed to follow up the victory.

Major General McClellan   Executive Mansion,
My dear Sir   Washington, Oct. 13, 1862.

You remember my speaking to you of what I called your over-cautiousness. Are you not over-cautious when you assume that you can not do what the enemy is constantly doing? Should you not claim to be at least his equal in prowess, and act upon the claim?

As I understand, you telegraph Gen. Halleck that you can not subsist your army at Winchester unless the Railroad from Harper's Ferry to that point be put in working order. But the enemy does now subsist his army at Winchester at a distance nearly twice as great from railroad transportation as you would have to do without the railroad last named. He now wagons from Culpepper C.H. which is just about twice as far as you would have to do from Harper's Ferry. He is certainly not more than half as well provided with wagons as you are. I certainly should be pleased for you to have the advantage of the Railroad from Harper's Ferry to Winchester, but it wastes all the remainder of autumn to give it to you; and, in fact ignores the question of *time,* which can not, and must not be ignored.

Again, one of the standard maxims of war, as you know, is "to operate upon the enemy's communications as much as possible without exposing your own." You seem to act as if this applies *against* you, but can not apply in your *favor.* Change positions with the enemy, and think you not he would break your communication with Richmond within the next twenty four hours? You dread his going into Pennsylvania. But if he does so in full force, he gives up his communications to you absolutely, and you have nothing to do but to follow, and ruin him; if he does so with less than full force, fall upon, and beat what is left behind all the easier. . . .

You know I desired, but did not order, you to cross the Potomac below, instead of above the Shenandoah and Blue Ridge. My idea was that this would at once menace the enemies' communications, which I would seize if he would permit. If he should move Northward I would follow him closely, holding his communications. If he should prevent our seizing his communications, and move towards Richmond, I would press closely to him, fight him if a favorable opportunity should present, and, at least, try to beat him to Richmond on the inside track. I say "try"; if we never try, we shall never succeed. If he make a stand at Winchester, moving neither North or South, I would fight him there, on the idea that if we can not beat him when he bears the wastage of coming to us, we never can when we bear the wastage of going to him. This proposition is a simple truth, and is too important to be lost sight of for a moment. In coming to us, he tenders us an advantage which we should not waive. We should not so operate as to merely drive him away. As we must beat him somewhere, or fail finally, we can do it, if at all, easier near to us, than far away. If we can not beat the enemy where he now is, we never can, he again being within the entrenchments of Richmond. . . .

I should think it preferable to take the route nearest the enemy, disabling him to make an important move without your knowledge, and compelling him to keep his forces together, for dread of you. The gaps would enable you to attack if you should wish. For a great part of the way, you would be practically between the enemy and both Washington and Richmond, enabling us to spare you the greatest number of troops from here. When at length, running for Richmond ahead of him enables him to move this way; if he does so, turn and attack him in rear. But I think he should be engaged long before such point is reached. It is all easy if our troops march as well as the enemy; and it is unmanly to say they can not do it.

This letter is in no sense an order.

Yours truly
A. LINCOLN.

Washington City, D.C.
Majr. Genl. McClellan   Oct. 24 [25]. 1862

I have just read your despatch about sore tongued and fateigued horses. Will you pardon me for asking what the horses of your army have done since the battle of Antietam that fatigue anything?

A. LINCOLN

LETTER TO GENERAL HOOKER, 1863

In November 1862, Lincoln replaced McClellan as commander of the Army of the Potomac with Ambrose E. Burnside. After the defeat at Fredericksburg in December, Burnside was replaced by Joseph Hooker, who had a reputation as an intriguer.

Major General Hooker: Executive Mansion,
General.   Washington, January 26, 1863.

I have placed you at the head of the Army of the Potomac. Of course I have done this upon what appear to me to be sufficient reasons. And yet I think it best for you to know that there are some things in regard to which, I am not quite satisfied with you. I believe you to be a brave and a skilful soldier, which, of course, I like. I also believe you do not mix politics with your profession, in which you are right. You have confidence in yourself, which is a valuable, if not an indispensable quality. You are ambitious, which, within reasonable bounds, does good rather than harm. But I think that during Gen. Burnside's command of the Army, you have taken counsel of your ambition, and thwarted him as much as you could, in which you did a great wrong to the country, and to a most meritorious and honorable brother officer. I have heard, in such way as to believe it, of your recently saying that both the Army and the Government needed a Dictator. Of course it was not *for* this, but in spite of it, that I have given you the command. Only those generals who gain successes, can set up dictators. What I now ask of you is military success, and I will risk the dictatorship. The government will support you to the utmost of it's ability, which is neither more nor less than it has done and will do for all commanders. I much fear that the spirit which you have aided to infuse into the Army, of criticising their Commander, and withholding confidence from him, will now turn upon you. I shall assist you as far as I can, to put it down. Neither you, nor Napoleon, if he were alive again, could get any good out of an army, while such a spirit prevails in it.

And now, beware of rashness. Beware of rashness, but with energy, and sleepless vigilance, go forward, and give us victories.   Yours very truly
                                                                                    A. LINCOLN

LETTER TO GENERAL GRANT, 1863

Lincoln seems greatly relieved to be addressing a general who is neither neurotic nor incompetent.

Major General Grant   Executive Mansion,
My dear General   Washington, July 13, 1863.
      I do not remember that you and I ever met personally. I write this now as a grateful acknowledgment for the almost inestimable service you have done the country. I wish to say a word further. When you first reached the vicinity of Vicksburg, I thought you should do, what you finally did—march the troops across the neck, run the batteries with the transports, and thus go below; and I never had any faith, except a general hope that you knew better than I, that the Yazoo Pass expedition, and the like, could succeed. When you got below, and took Port-Gibson, Grand Gulf, and vicinity, I thought you should go down the river and join Gen. Banks; and when you turned Northward East of the Big Black, I feared it was a mistake. I now wish to make the personal acknowledgment that you were right, and I was wrong.   Yours very truly
                                                                                    A. LINCOLN

LETTER TO GENERAL GRANT, 1864

Another note, free of coaxing or coercive flattery, to the commander who had won Lincoln's complete trust.

Executive Mansion Washington,
Lieutenant General Grant.   April 30, 1864

    Not expecting to see you again before the Spring campaign opens, I wish to express, in this way, my entire satisfaction with what you have done up to this time, so far as I understand it. The particulars of your plans I neither know, or seek to know. You are vigilant and self-reliant; and, pleased with this, I wish not to obtrude any constraints or restraints upon you. While I am very anxious that any great disaster, or the capture of our men in great numbers, shall be avoided, I know these points are less likely to escape your attention than they would be mine. If there is anything wanting which is within my power to give, do not fail to let me know it.

    And now with a brave Army, and a just cause, may God sustain you.   Yours very truly
A. Lincoln

LETTER TO GENERAL SHERMAN, 1864

Sherman's capture of Atlanta played a part in Lincoln's reelection in November, and now the general offered Savannah to Lincoln as a "Christmas-gift."

Executive Mansion, Washington,
My dear General Sherman.   Dec. 26, 1864.

Many, many, thanks for your Christmas-gift—the capture of Savannah.

When you were about leaving Atlanta for the Atlantic coast, I was *anxious,* if not fearful; but feeling that you were the better judge, and remembering that "nothing risked, nothing gained" I did not interfere. Now, the undertaking being a success, the honor is all yours; for I believe none of us went farther than to acquiesce. And, taking the work of Gen. Thomas into the count, as it should be taken, it is indeed a great success. Not only does it afford the obvious and immediate military advantages; but, in showing to the world that your army could be divided, putting the stronger part to an important new service, and yet leaving enough to vanquish the old opposing force of the whole—Hood's army—it brings those who sat in darkness, to see a great light. But what next? I suppose it will be safer if I leave Gen. Grant and yourself to decide.

Please make my grateful acknowledgments to your whole army, officers and men.   Yours very truly
A. LINCOLN.

Full-length portrait of Abraham Lincoln, November 8, 1863. Albumen photograph by Alexander Gardner.
(Courtesy of the Library of Congress, LC-DIG-ppmsca-19191)

VI. "I Am Not a Very Sentimental Man": The Human Comedy and the Game of Politics

TO C. U. SCHLATER
January 5, 1849

Your note, requesting my "signature with a sentiment" was received, and should have been answered long since, but that it was mislaid. I am not a very sentimental man; and the best sentiment I can think of is, that if you collect the signatures of all persons who are no less distinguished than I, you will have a very undistinguishing mass of names.

Very respectfully
A. LINCOLN

SPEECH IN THE ILLINOIS LEGISLATURE CONCERNING THE STATE BANK
January 11, 1837

The young legislator takes on an opponent who declared that he didn't want to waste ammunition on small game.

In one faculty, at least, there can be no dispute of the gentleman's superiority over me, and most other men; and that is, the faculty of entangling a subject, so that neither himself, or any other man, can find head or tail to it. Here he has introduced a resolution, embracing ninety-nine printed lines across common writing paper, and yet more than one half of his opening speech has been made upon subjects about which there is not one word said in his resolution.

Mr. Chairman, this movement is exclusively the work of politicians; a set of men who have interests aside from the interests of the people, and who, to say the most of them, are, taken as a mass, at least one long step removed from honest men. I say this with the greater freedom because, being a politician myself, none can regard it as personal.

LETTER TO JOSHUA SPEED
February 25, 1842

My old Father used to have a saying that "If you make a bad bargain, hug it the tighter."

SPEECH IN THE U.S. HOUSE OF REPRESENTA-TIVES ON THE PRESIDENTIAL QUESTION
July 27, 1848

A fellow once advertised that he had made a discovery by which he could make a new man out of an old one, and have enough of the stuff left to make a little yellow dog. Just such a discovery has Gen. Jackson's popularity been to you. You not only twice made President of him out of it, but you have had enough of the stuff left, to make Presidents of several comparatively small men since; and it is your chief reliance now to make still another.

By the way, Mr. Speaker, did you know I am a military hero? Yes sir; in the days of the Black Hawk war, I fought, bled, and came away. Speaking of Gen. Cass' career, reminds me of my own. I was not at Stillman's defeat, but I was about as near it, as Cass was to Hulls surrender; and, like him, I saw the place very soon afterwards. It is quite certain I did not break my sword, for I had none to break; but I bent a musket pretty badly on one occasion. If Cass broke his sword, the idea is, he broke it in de[s]peration; I bent the musket by accident. If Gen. Cass went in advance of me in picking huckleberries [whortleberries], I guess I surpassed him in charges upon the wild onions. If he saw any live, fighting indians, it was more than I did; but I had a good many bloody struggles with the musquetoes; and, although I never fainted from loss of blood, I can truly say I was often very hungry.

I have heard some things from New-York; and if they are true, one might well say of your party there, as a drunken fellow once said when he heard the reading of an indictment for hog-stealing. The clerk read on till he got to, and through the words "did steal, take, and carry away, ten boars, ten sows, ten shoats, and ten pigs" at which he exclaimed "Well, by golly, that is the most equally divided gang of hogs, I ever did hear of." If there is any other gang of hogs more equally divided than the democrats of NewYork are about this time, I have not heard of it.

SPEECH TO THE SPRINGFIELD SCOTT CLUB
August 14, 1852

Gen. Pierce has been in the State Legislature and in congress; and I misread his history if it does not show him to have had just sufficient capacity, and no more, of setting his foot down in the track, as his partizan leader lifted his out of it—and so trudging along in the party team without a single original tho't or independent action.

TWO EXCERPTS FROM THE FIRST LINCOLN-DOUGLAS DEBATE, OTTAWA, ILLINOIS
August 21, 1858
Note: A "grocery" was a tavern or liquor store.

The Judge is wofully at fault about his early friend Lincoln being a "grocery keeper." [Laughter.] I don't know as it would be a great sin, if I had been, but he is mistaken. Lincoln never kept a grocery anywhere in the world. [Laughter.] It is true that Lincoln did work the latter part of one winter in a small still house, up at the head of a hollow. [Roars of laughter.] . . .

As I have not used up so much of my time as I had supposed, I will dwell a little longer upon one or two of these minor topics upon which the Judge has spoken. He has read from my speech in Springfield, in which I say that "a house divided against itself cannot stand." Does the Judge say it *can* stand? [Laughter.] I don't know whether he does or not. The Judge does not seem to be attending to me just now, but I would like to know if it is his opinion that a house divided against itself *can stand.* If he does, then there is a question of veracity, not between him and me, but between the Judge and an authority of a somewhat higher character. [Laughter and applause.]...

TO DANIEL P. GARDNER
September 28, 1860

Some specimens of your Soap have been used at our house and Mrs. L. declares it is a superb article. She at the same time, protests that I have never given sufficient attention to the "soap question" to be a competent judge.

Yours truly
A. LINCOLN

FROM GRACE BEDELL TO ABRAHAM LINCOLN AND HIS REPLY
October 15, 1860

My father has just home from the fair and brought home your picture and Mr. Hamlin's. I am a little girl only eleven years old, but want you should be President of the United States very much so I hope you wont think me very bold to write to such a great man as you are. Have you any little girls about as large as I am if so give them my love and tell her to write to me if you cannot answer this letter. I have got 4 brother's and part of them will vote for you any way and if you will let your whiskers grow I will try and get the rest of them to vote for you you would look a great deal better for your face is so thin. All the ladies like whiskers and they would tease their husband's to vote for you and then you would be President. My father is a going to vote for you and if I was a man I would vote for you to but I will try and get every one to vote for you that I can I think that rail fence around your picture makes it look very pretty I have got a little baby sister she is nine weeks old and is just as cunning as can be. When you direct your letter dir[e]ct to Grace Bedell Westfield Chatauque County New York.

I must not write any more answer this letter right off Good bye.

OCTOBER 19, 1860

Miss. Grace Bedell Springfield, Ills.
My dear little Miss.

Your very agreeable letter of the 15th. is received.

I regret the necessity of saying I have no daughters. I have three sons—one seventeen, one nine, and one seven, years of age. They, with their mother, constitute my whole family.

As to the whiskers, having never worn any, do you not think people would call it a piece of silly affection if I were to begin it now?

Your very sincere well-wisher
A. LINCOLN.

LETTER TO SIMON CAMERON
January 3, 1861

My dear Sir Since seeing you things have developed which make it impossible for me to take you into the cabinet. You will say this comes of an interview

with McClure; and this is partly, but not wholly
true. The more potent matter is wholly outside of
Pennsylvania; and yet I am not at liberty to specify
it. Enough that it appears to me to be sufficient.
And now I suggest that you write me declining the
appointment, in which case I do not object to its
being known that it was tendered you. Better do this
at once, before things so change, that you can not
honorably decline, and I be compelled to openly
recall the tender. No person living knows, or has an
intimation that I write this letter.
P.S. Telegraph, me instantly, on receipt of this, saying "All right"   A. L.

REMARKS AT THE MONONGAHELA HOUSE, PITTSBURGH, PA
February 14, 1861

You know that it has not been my custom, since I
started on the route to Washington, to make long
speeches; I am rather inclined to silence, and
whether that be wise or not, it is at least more
unusual now-a-days to find a man who can hold his
tongue than to find one who cannot.

LETTER TO THURLOW WEED
February 4, 1861

My dear Sir. I have both your letter to myself, and
that to Judge Davis, in relation to a certain gentle-

man in your state claiming to dispense patronage in my name, and also to be authorized to use my name to advance the chances of Mr. Greely for an election to the U.S. Senate. It is very strange that such things should be said by any one. The gentleman you mention, did speak to me of Mr. Greely, in connection with the Senatorial election, and I replied in terms of kindness towards Mr. Greely which I really feel, but always with an express protest that my name must not be used in the Senatorial election, in favor of, or against any one. Any other representation of me, is a misrepresentation.

As to the matter of dispensing patronage, it perhaps will surprise you to learn, that I have information that you claim to have my authority to arrange that matter in N.Y. I do not believe you have so claimed; but still so some men say. On that subject you know all I have said to you is "justice to all", and I beg you to believe I have said nothing more particular to any one. I say this to re-assure you that I have not changed my purpose; in the hope however, that you will not use my name in the matter).

FROM A LETTER TO JAMES H. HACKETT
August 17, 1863
Hackett was a leading American actor whose most famous role was Falstaff.

For one of my age, I have seen very little of the drama. The first presentation of Falstaff I ever saw was yours here, last winter or spring. Perhaps the best compliment I can pay is to say, as I truly can, I am very anxious to see it again. Some of Shakspeare's plays I have never read; while others I have gone over perhaps as frequently as any unprofessional reader. Among the latter are Lear, Richard Third, Henry Eighth, Hamlet, and especially Macbeth. I think nothing equals Macbeth. It is wonderful. Unlike you gentlemen of the profession, I think the soliloquy in Hamlet commencing "O, my offence is rank" surpasses that commencing "To be, or not to be." But pardon this small attempt at criticism. I should like to hear you pronounce the opening speech of Richard the Third. Will you not soon visit Washington again? If you do, please call and let me make your personal acquaintance.

FROM A LETTER TO JAMES H. HACKETT
November 2, 1863

My note to you I certainly did not expect to see in print; yet I have not been much shocked by the newspaper comments upon it. Those comments constitute a fair specimen of what has occurred to me through life. I have endured a great deal of ridicule without much malice; and have received a great deal of kindness, not quite free from ridicule. I am used to it.

Portrait of Abraham Lincoln holding his spectacles, Gardner's Gallery, Washington, D.C., February 5, 1865. Photograph by Alexander Gardner. *(Courtesy of the Library of Congress, LC-USZ61-1938)*

VII. "The Fiery Trial Through Which We Pass"

FROM THE ANNUAL MESSAGE TO CONGRESS
December 1, 1862
In September 1861, McClellan had turned back the Con-
federate invasion of Maryland at Antietam, and Lincoln
seized the opportunity to issue a preliminary emancipation
order. Thereafter, as the Confederate military threat re-
ceded, Lincoln spoke more of the evils of slavery and of the
war as an occasion to root out a historical evil. He spoke
less in terms of a political mission and more of a spiritual
mission.

The dogmas of the quiet past, are inadequate to the
stormy present. The occasion is piled high with
difficulty, and we must rise with the occasion. As
our case is new, so we must think anew, and act
anew. We must disenthrall our selves, and then we
shall save our country.

Fellow-citizens, *we* cannot escape history. We of
this Congress and this administration, will be re-
membered in spite of ourselves. No personal significance, or insignificance, can spare one or another of
us. The fiery trial through which we pass, will light
us down, in honor or dishonor, to the latest generation. We *say* we are for the Union. The world will
not forget that we say this. We know how to save
the Union. The world knows we do know how to
save it. We—even *we here*—hold the power, and bear
the responsibility. In *giving* freedom to the *slave,* we
assure freedom to the *free*—honorable alike in what

we give, and what we preserve. We shall nobly save, or meanly lose, the last best, hope of earth. Other means may succeed; this could not fail. The way is plain, peaceful, generous, just—a way which, if followed, the world will forever applaud, and God must forever bless.

EMANCIPATION PROCLAMATION, 1863

The Emancipation Proclamation had little immediate practical effect in liberating slaves, but it was of great symbolic import in declaring that emancipation was to be a central goal of the war.

JANUARY 1, 1863

By the President of the United States of America:

A Proclamation.

Whereas, on the twentysecond day of September, in the year of our Lord one thousand eight hundred and sixty two, a proclamation was issued by the President of the United States, containing, among other things, the following, towit:

That on the first day of January, in the year of our Lord one thousand eight hundred and sixty-three, all persons held as slaves within any State or designated part of a State, the people whereof shall then be in rebellion against the United States, shall be then, thenceforward, and forever free; and the Executive Government of the United States, including the military and naval authority thereof, will recognize and maintain the freedom of such persons, and will do no act or acts to repress such persons, or any of them, in any efforts they may make for their actual freedom.

That the Executive will, on the first day of January aforesaid, by proclamation, designate the States and parts of States, if any, in which the people thereof, respectively, shall then be in rebellion against the United States; and the fact that any State, or the people thereof, shall on that day be, in good faith, represented in the Congress of the United States by members chosen thereto at elections wherein a majority of the qualified voters of such State shall have participated, shall, in the absence of strong countervailing testimony, be deemed conclusive evidence that such State, and the people thereof, are not then in rebellion against the United States.

Now, therefore I, Abraham Lincoln, President of the United States, by virtue of the power in me vested as Commander-in-Chief, of the Army and Navy of the United States in time of actual armed rebellion against authority and government of the United States, and as a fit and necessary war measure for suppressing said rebellion, do, on this first day of January, in the year of our Lord one thousand eight hundred and sixty three, and in accordance with my purpose so to do publicly proclaimed for the full period of one hundred days, from the day first above mentioned, order and designate as the States and parts of States wherein the people thereof respectively, are this day in rebellion against the United States, the following, towit:

Arkansas, Texas, Louisiana, (except the Parishes of St. Bernard, Plaquemines, Jefferson, St. Johns, St. Charles, St. James [,] Ascension, Assumption, Terrebonne, Lefourche, St. Mary, St. Martin, and Orleans, including the City of New-Orleans) Mississippi, Alabama, Florida, Georgia, South-Carolina, North-Carolina, and Virginia, (except the fortyeight counties designated as West Virginia, and also the counties of Berkley, Accomac, Northampton, Elizabeth-City, York, Princess Ann, and Norfolk, including the cities of Norfolk & Portsmouth [)]; and which excepted parts are, for the present, left precisely as if this proclamation were not issued.

And by virtue of the power, and for the purpose aforesaid, I do order and declare that all persons held as slaves within said designated States, and parts of States, are, and henceforward shall be free; and that the Executive government of the United States, including the military and naval authorities thereof, will recognize and maintain the freedom of said persons.

And I hereby enjoin upon the people so declared to be free to abstain from all violence, unless in necessary self-defence; and I recommend to them that, in all cases when allowed, they labor faithfully for reasonable wages.

And I further declare and make known, that such persons of suitable condition, will be received into the armed service of the United States to garrison forts, positions, stations, and other places, and to man vessels of all sorts in said service.

And upon this act, sincerely believed to be an act of justice, warranted by the Constitution, upon military necessity, I invoke the considerate judgment of mankind, and the gracious favor of Almighty God.

In witness whereof, I have hereunto set my hand and caused the seal of the United States to be affixed.

Done at the City of Washington, this first day of January, in the year of our Lord one thousand eight hundred and sixty three, and of the Independence of the United States of America the eighty-seventh.
By the President: ABRAHAM LINCOLN
WILLIAM H. SEWARD, Secretary of State.

FROM A LETTER TO JAMES C. CONKLING
August 26, 1863

Thanks to all. For the great republic—for the principle it lives by, and keeps alive—for man's vast future, —thanks to all.

Peace does not appear so distant as it did. I hope it will come soon, and come to stay; and so come as to be worth the keeping in all future time. It will then have been proved that, among free men, there can be no successful appeal from the ballot to the bullet; and that they who take such appeal are sure to lose their case, and pay the cost. And then, there will be some black men who can remember that, with silent tongue, and clenched teeth, and steady eye, and well-poised bayonet, they have helped mankind on to this great consummation; while, I fear, there will be some white ones, unable to forget that, with malignant heart, and deceitful speech, they have strove to hinder it.

REMARKS TO BALTIMORE PRESBYTERIAN SYNOD, WASHINGTON, D.C.
October 24, 1863

I sincerely wish that I was a more devoted man than I am. Sometimes in my difficulties I have been driven to the last resort to say God is still my only hope. It is still all the world to me.

THE GETTYSBURG ADDRESS
November 19, 1863

Edward Everett, the leading orator of the day, was invited to make the principal address at the ceremonies dedicating the national cemetery. President Lincoln was asked to make a few concluding remarks (it was hoped he wouldn't sully the occasion by telling funny stories). Everett's address lasted two hours, but Lincoln's remarks, which he had prepared with great care, were over almost before the audience had begun to listen—it was said that a man with a cam-

era didn't have time to set up his equipment before Lincoln was finished. Nobody who was there seemed to feel that he had heard a masterpiece of oratory.

Four score and seven years ago our fathers brought forth on this continent, a new nation, conceived in Liberty, and dedicated to the proposition that all men are created equal.

Now we are engaged in a great civil war, testing whether that nation, or any nation so conceived and so dedicated, can long endure. We are met on a great battle-field of that war. We have come to dedicate a portion of that field, as a final resting place for those who here gave their lives that that nation might live. It is altogether fitting and proper that we should do this.

But, in a larger sense, we can not dedicate—we can not consecrate—we can not hallow—this ground. The brave men, living and dead, who struggled here, have consecrated it, far above our poor power to add or detract. The world will little note, nor long remember what we say here, but it can never forget what they did here. It is for us the living, rather, to be dedicated here to the unfinished work which they who fought here have thus far so nobly advanced. It is rather for us to be here dedicated to the great task remaining before us—that from these honored dead we take increased devotion to that cause for which they gave the last full measure of devotion—that we here highly resolve that these dead shall not have died in vain—that this nation, under God, shall have a new birth of freedom—and that government of the people, by the people, for the people, shall not perish from the earth.

FROM A LETTER TO EDWARD EVERETT
November 20, 1863

Your kind note of to-day is received. In our respective parts yesterday, you could not have been excused to make a short address, nor I a long one. I am pleased to know that, in your judgment, the little I did say was not entirely a failure.

ENDORSEMENT CONCERNING HENRY ANDREWS
January 7, 1864

The case of Andrews is really a very bad one, as appears by the record already before me. Yet before receiving this I had ordered his punishment commuted to imprisonment for during the war at hard labor, and had so telegraphed. I did this, not on any merit in the case, but because I am trying to evade the butchering business lately.

FROM A LETTER TO EDWARD M. STANTON
February 5, 1864

On principle I dislike an oath which requires a man to swear he has not done wrong. It rejects the Christian principle of forgiveness on terms of repentance. I think it is enough if the man does no wrong hereafter.

REMARKS AT CLOSING OF SANITARY FAIR, WASHINGTON, D.C.
March 18, 1864

I am not accustomed to the use of language of eulogy; I have never studied the art of paying compliments to women; but I must say that if all that has been said by orators and poets since the creation of the world in praise of woman were applied to the women of America, it would not do them justice for their conduct during this war.

FROM A LETTER TO A. G. HODGES
April 4, 1864

I claim not to have controlled events, but confess plainly that events have controlled me. Now, at the end of three years struggle the nation's condition is not what either party, or any man devised, or expected. God alone can claim it. Whither it is tending seems plain. If God now wills the removal of a great wrong, and wills also that we of the North as well as you of the South, shall pay fairly for our complicity in that wrong, impartial history will find therein new cause to attest and revere the justice and goodness of God.

FROM A LETTER TO GEORGE B. IDE, JAMES R. DOOLITTLE, AND A. HUBBELL
May 30, 1864

When, a year or two ago, those professedly holy men of the South, met in the semblance of prayer and devotion, and, in the name of Him who said "As ye would all men should do unto you, do ye even so unto them" appealed to the christian world to aid them in doing to a whole race of men, as they would have no man do unto themselves, to my thinking, they contemned and insulted God and His church, far more than did Satan when he tempted the Saviour with the Kingdoms of the earth. The devils attempt was no more false, and far less hypocritical. But let me forbear, remembering it is also written "Judge not, lest ye be judged."

RESPONSE TO A SERENADE
November 10, 1864

What has occurred in this case, must ever recur in similar cases. Human-nature will not change. In any future great national trial, compared with the men of this, we shall have as weak, and as strong; as silly and as wise; as bad and good. Let us, therefore, study the incidents of this, as philosophy to learn wisdom from, and none of them as wrongs to be revenged.

SECOND INAUGURAL ADDRESS, 1865

The First Inaugural had been built of reasons and argument, like a lawyer's summation to a jury. At the Second Inaugural the time for argument was past, and Lincoln addressed the nation not as its commander-in-chief but as its spiritual leader.

[Fellow Countrymen:]   March 4, 1865

At this second appearing to take the oath of the presidential office, there is less occasion for an extended address than there was at the first. Then a statement, somewhat in detail, of a course to be pursued, seemed fitting and proper. Now, at the expiration of four years, during which public declarations have been constantly called forth on every point and phase of the great contest which still absorbs the attention, and engrosses the enerergies [sic] of the nation, little that is new could be presented. The progress of our arms, upon which all else chiefly depends, is as well known to the public as to myself; and it is, I trust, reasonably satisfactory and encouraging to all. With high hope for the future, no prediction in regard to it is ventured.

On the occasion corresponding to this four years ago, all thoughts were anxiously directed to an impending civil-war. All dreaded it—all sought to avert it. While the inaugural address was being delivered from this place, devoted altogether to saving the Union without war, insurgent agents were in the city seeking to destroy it without war— seeking to dissol[v]e the Union, and divide effects, by negotiation. Both parties deprecated war; but one of them would make war rather than let the nation survive; and the other would accept war rather than let it perish. And the war came.

One eighth of the whole population were colored slaves, not distributed generally over the Union, but localized in the Southern part of it. These slaves constituted a peculiar and powerful interest. All knew that this interest was, somehow, the cause of the war. To strengthen, perpetuate, and extend this interest was the object for which the insurgents would rend the Union, even by war; while the government claimed no right to do more than to restrict the territorial enlargement of it. Neither party expected for the war, the magnitude, or the duration, which it has already attained. Neither anticipated that the cause of the conflict might cease with, or even before, the conflict itself should cease. Each looked for an easier triumph, and a result less fundamental and astounding. Both read the same Bible, and pray to the same God; and each invokes

His aid against the other. It may seem strange that any men should dare to ask a just God's assistance in wringing their bread from the sweat of other men's faces; but let us judge not that we be not judged. The prayers of both could not be answered; that of neither has been answered fully. The Almighty has His own purposes, "Woe unto the world because of offences! for it must needs be that offences come; but woe to that man by whom the offence cometh!" If we shall suppose that American Slavery is one of those offences which, in the providence of God, must needs come, but which, having continued through His appointed time, He now wills to remove, and that He gives to both North and South, this terrible war, as the woe due to those by whom the offence came, shall we discern therein any departure from those divine attributes which the believers in a Living God always ascribe to Him? Fondly do we hope—fervently do we pray—that this mighty scourge of war may speedily pass away. Yet, if God wills that it continue, until all the wealth piled by the bond-man's two hundred and fifty years of unrequited toil shall be sunk, and until every drop of blood drawn with the lash, shall be paid by another drawn with the sword, as was said three thousand years ago, so still it must be said "the judgments of the Lord, are true and righteous altogether"

With malice toward none; with charity for all; with firmness in the right, as God gives us to see the right, let us strive on to finish the work we are in; to bind up the nation's wounds; to care for him who shall have borne the battle, and for his widow, and his orphan—to do all which may achieve and cherish a just, and lasting peace, among ourselves, and with all nations.

FROM A LETTER TO THURLOW WEED
March 15, 1865

Every one likes a compliment. Thank you for yours on my little notification speech, and on the recent Inaugeral Address. I expect the latter to wear as well as—perhaps better than—any thing I have produced; but I believe it is not immediately popular. Men are not flattered by being shown that there has been a difference of purpose between the Almighty and them. To deny it, however, in this case, is to deny that there is a God governing the world. It is a truth which I thought needed to be told; and as whatever of humiliation there is in it, falls most directly on myself, I thought others might afford for me to tell it.

FROM THE LAST PUBLIC ADDRESS
April 11, 1865
Lincoln's last public remarks were an attempt to explain what he was trying to do to bring the South back into the nation, using Louisiana as an example. It is said that

John Wilkes Booth was in the audience and left in a rage over what he heard.

Some twelve thousand voters in the heretofore slave-state of Louisiana have sworn allegiance to the Union, assumed to be the rightful political power of the State, held elections, organized a State government, adopted a free-state constitution, giving the benefit of public schools equally to black and white, and empowering the Legislature to confer the elective franchise upon the colored man. Their Legislature has already voted to ratify the constitutional amendment recently passed by Congress, abolishing slavery throughout the nation. These twelve thousand persons are thus fully committed to the Union, and to perpetual freedom in the state— committed to the very things, and nearly all the things the nation wants—and they ask the nations recognition, and it's assistance to make good their committal. Now, if we reject, and spurn them, we do our utmost to disorganize and disperse them. We in effect say to the white men "You are worthless, or worse—we will neither help you, nor be helped by you." To the blacks we say "This cup of liberty which these, your old masters, hold to your lips, we will dash from you, and leave you to the chances of gathering the spilled and scattered contents in some vague and undefined when, where, and how." If this course, discouraging and paralyzing both white and black, has any tendency to bring Louisiana into proper practical relations with the Union, I have, so far, been unable to perceive it. If, on the contrary, we recognize, and sustain the new government of Louisiana the converse of all this is made true. We encourage the hearts, and nerve the arms of the twelve thousand to adhere to their work, and argue for it, and proselyte for it, and fight for it, and feed it, and grow it, and ripen it to a complete success. The colored man too, in seeing all united for him, is inspired with vigilance, and energy, and daring, to the same end. Grant that he desires the elective franchise, will he not attain it sooner by saving the already advanced steps toward it, than by running backward over them? Concede that the new government of Louisiana is only to what it should be as the egg is to the fowl, we shall sooner have the fowl by hatching the egg than by smashing it?

CHRONOLOGY

1809 Born February 12 in a log cabin south of present-day Hodgenville in Hardin County, Kentucky. Second child of farmer Thomas Lincoln and Nancy Hanks Lincoln. (Sister Sarah born in 1807.)

1815 Attends school briefly.

1816 Attends school briefly in the fall. Family moves to Indiana in December.

1818 Nancy Hanks Lincoln dies during an epidemic of milk sickness.

1819 Thomas Lincoln marries Sarah Bush Johnston, a widow with three children.

1820 Attends school briefly.

1824 Works on family farm and hires out to neighbors. Attends school in fall and winter. Reading includes the Bible, Weems's biography of Washington, *Robinson Crusoe, Pilgrim's Progress, Aesop's Fables,* and a history of the United States.

1828 Sister Sarah dies in childbirth. Lincoln and a neighborhood boy take a cargo of local crops on a flatboat down the Mississippi to sell in New Orleans.

1830 The family moves to Macon County, Illinois. Lincoln speaks at a meeting in favor of navigation improvements on the Sangamon River—his first public speech.

1831   Second flatboat trip to New Orleans to sell hogs and corn. Moves to New Salem, Illinois, to work in a general store, where he sleeps in the back room. Joins debating society, reads Shakespeare. Meets tavern owner James Rutledge and his daughter, Ann.

1832   Volunteers for state militia during Black Hawk War, does not see action. Becomes partner in a general store. Runs for Illinois House of Representatives, loses.

1833   General store fails, leaving Lincoln in debt. Works as postmaster and deputy county surveyor.

1832   Elected to Illinois House of Representatives as member of the Whig party. Begins to study law. Meets Stephen A. Douglas.

1835   Ann Rutledge dies.

1836   Wins re-election to Illinois House and earns license to practice law.

1837   Moves to Springfield when the state capitol is moved there from Vandalia. Becomes law partner with John T. Stuart, who had lent him law books during his period of study. His marriage proposal to Mary Owens is rejected. Lives with store owner Joshua Speed, who would become a close friend.

1839   Meets Mary Todd, cousin of his law partner John T. Stuart and daughter of a Kentucky banker.

1840   Becomes engaged to Mary Todd. Argues first case before Illinois Supreme Court, debates Stephen Douglas in the course of campaigning for Whig presidential candidate William Henry Harrison.

CHRONOLOGY

1841 Breaks off his engagement to Mary Todd, suffers incapacitating depression.

1842 Does not run for re-election to Illinois House. Nearly fights a duel with broadswords. Becomes engaged to Mary Todd again, and they marry on November 4.

1843 Robert Todd Lincoln born. He would be the only Lincoln child to live to maturity.

1844 Buys a house in Springfield and opens a law practice with William D. Herndon as his junior partner.

1846 Elected to U.S. House of Representatives on the Whig party ticket. Son Edward Baker Lincoln is born.

1847 Moves to a boarding house in Washington, D.C., to begin his term as congressman.

1848 Speaks out against Mexican War policy of President Polk in the House.

1849 Votes to abolish slavery in the District of Columbia and U.S. territories, but does not participate in House debate. Does not run for re-election. Returns to practice law in Illinois.

1850 Son Edward dies after lingering illness. Son William Wallace ("Willie") is born.

1852 Mary joins First Presbyterian Church in Springfield, which Lincoln attends occasionally without becoming a member.

1853 Son Thomas ("Tad") is born.

1854 Congress passes the Kansas-Nebraska Act, canceling the Missouri Compromise on the extension of slavery—and Lincoln's interest in politics is rekindled. Speaks out against the new law and its primary sponsor, Stephen A. Douglas.

1856 Helps found the Republican party in Illinois and makes more than 50 speeches on behalf of its presidential candidate, John C. Frémont.

1858 Unsuccessful campaign to unseat Stephen A. Douglas in the U.S. Senate, highlighted by the Lincoln-Douglas debates across the state.

1860 Delivers speech on slavery as a threat to the American nation at the Cooper Union in New York, continues speaking throughout the Northeast. Nominated as Republican candidate for president at the party convention in Chicago. (Four of his rivals for the nomination will receive appointments to his Cabinet.) In a four-way contest for the presidency on November 6, wins a 40% plurality and 180 of 303 electoral votes. On December 20, South Carolina secedes from the Union.

1861 Inaugurated on March 4. Sends naval resupply expedition to Fort Sumter in Charleston, S.C., harbor. Within weeks, eleven Southern states secede from the Union. Appoints George B. McClellan commander of the Army of the Potomac and, soon after, commander of the Union Army. Uses the War Department telegraph office to monitor progress of the Battle of Bull Run, a practice he will continue.

CHRONOLOGY

1862 Wrangles with General McClellan over conduct of the war and takes direct command of the Union Army. Defends newly promoted General Grant after defeat at Shiloh. Following victory at Antietam, issues preliminary Emancipation Proclamation. Son Willie dies.

1863 Issues Emancipation Proclamation on January 1, freeing slaves in Confederate states. As Lee approaches Pennsylvania in late June, replaces General Hooker with General Meade to hold Lee back at Gettysburg. Receives Frederick Douglass at the White House to discuss recruitment of black soldiers. Delivers short dedication speech at Gettysburg Cemetery.

1864 Appoints Grant general-in-chief of the armies, with Sherman replacing Grant in command of the western armies. Sherman's success at Atlanta improves Lincoln's prospects for re-election. Wins re-election against his Democratic rival, former General George McClellan.

1865 Encourages Congress to advance an amendment to the Constitution abolishing slavery. Meets inconclusively with Confederate representatives. Tours Confederate capital of Richmond after withdrawal of Confederate Army. Returns to Washington as Lee surrenders to Grant at Appomattox. Shot by John Wilkes Booth on April 14 and dies the next day without recovering consciousness.

The Words of Abraham Lincoln have been selected by Larry Shapiro, former editor in chief of the Book-of-the-Month Club, former editorial director of the History Book Club, and author of *A Book of Days in American History.*

THE ACCLAIMED NEWMARKET *WORDS OF* SERIES

The Words of Abraham Lincoln
Selected and with an Introduction by Larry Shapiro

A collection of wise and inspiring quotations from the speeches and writings of Abraham Lincoln covering the slavery controversy, the Civil War, and his personal life. Includes photographs, chronology; 128 pages.

The Words of Albert Schweitzer
Selected and Introduced by Norman Cousins

An inspiring collection focusing on: Knowledge and Discovery, Reverence for Life, Faith, The Life of the Soul, The Musician as Artist, and Civilization and Peace. Includes photographs; chronology; excerpt from acceptance speech for Nobel Peace Prize, 1954; 112 pages.

The Words of Desmond Tutu
Selected and Introduced by Naomi Tutu

Nearly 100 memorable quotations from the addresses, sermons, and writings of South Africa's Nobel Prize–winning archbishop. Topics include: Faith and Responsibility, Apartheid, Family, Violence and Nonviolence, The Community—Black and White, and Toward a New South Africa. Includes photographs; chronology; text of acceptance speech for the Nobel Peace Prize, 1984; 112 pages.

The Words of Gandhi
Selected and with an Introduction by Richard Attenborough

More than 150 selections from the letters, speeches, and writings, collected in five sections—Daily Life, Cooperation, Nonviolence, Faith, and Peace. Includes *Time* magazine's millennium essay on Gandhi's impact on the twentieth century; photographs, chronology, bibliography, glossary; 128 pages.

The Words of Harry S Truman
Selected and Introduced by Robert J. Donovan

This volume of quotations from Truman's speeches and writings gives the essence of his views on politics, leadership, civil rights, war and peace, and "giving 'em hell." Includes photographs, chronology; 112 pages.

The Words of Martin Luther King, Jr.
Selected and Introduced by Coretta Scott King

More than 120 quotations and excerpts from the great civil rights leader's speeches, sermons, and writings on: The Community of Man, Racism, Civil Rights, Justice and Freedom, Faith and Religion, Nonviolence, and Peace. Includes photographs, chronology, text of presidential proclamation of King holiday; 128 pages.

The Words of Peace
Selections from the Speeches of the Winners of the Nobel Peace Prize
Edited by Professor Irwin Abrams. Foreword by President Jimmy Carter

A new compendium of excerpts from award winners' acceptance speeches spanning 1901 to 2007, including Al Gore, the Dalai Lama, Mother Teresa, Lech Walesa, Martin Luther King, Jr., and Elie Wiesel. Themes are: Peace, Human Rights, Violence and Nonviolence, The Bonds of Humanity, and Faith and Hope. Includes photographs, biographical notes, chronology, and index; 176 pages.

Newmarket Press books are available from your local bookseller or from Newmarket Press, Special Sales Department, 18 East 48th Street, New York, NY 10017; phone 212-832-3575 or 800-669-3903; fax 212-832-3629; e-mail info@newmarketpress.com. Prices and availability are subject to change. Catalogs and information on quantity order discounts are available on request.

www.newmarketpress.com